Peacock

Peacocks as pets

Peacock book for Care, Pros and Cons, Housing,
Diet and Health.

By

Jessy Langley

Table of Contents

Introduction

Although the term peacock is applied to a single bird, there are several terms that anyone interested in raising peafowl should be familiar with. One, peacock identifies the brilliant blue or green birds that we commonly known. Two, peafowl refers to any type of pea species or variety and includes both males and females. Three, peahens are the females in the peafowl species.

This book covers feeding, daily care, grooming, socializing and finally nesting and breeding your birds. It is a complete guide and is the only resource that you will need to successfully raise your own peafowl. This book also looks at all of the species of peafowl you can raise.

Today, many people can recall childhood memories of trips to zoos, and in those memories, the peacock, walking gracefully across the green or perching on a fence, is a prominent feature.

Of course, the first step in any type of journey is always discovering where you want to start and after researching peacocks, I realized that I could bring them into my own home.

The peacock is a beautiful creature and it is one that has captured the hearts and imaginations of people around the world. In fact, the peacock has been revered for millennia and even the Roman goddess Juno was linked to the bird. In her story, her chariot was drawn, not by horses, but by splendid peacocks, their colours flashing and eyes shining.

In addition, I realized that there was not a lot of information available to fans of the beautiful birds – information such as what to feed your birds, how to house them properly in all climates and how to ensure that your next generation of peafowl are healthier than your first. All of that information was missing for new enthusiasts to these creatures.

I have lost count of the number of peacocks I spied roaming around a zoo but for many years, I thought they were simply a bird that can only be found there. I didn't think that I would be able to bring it into my own home to grace my property.

It was that lack of information that influenced me to take my own understanding of peacocks and peafowl, but more specifically Peacocks, and turn it into an informative book that will answer all of your questions. Throughout this book, I have covered how to find the best breeder for your starting birds to how to bring those birds home.

In fact, raising peafowl and peacocks can be a very rewarding experience simply because of how amazing and gregarious these birds truly are. They are not an accessory, but a beautiful companion.

Literally, just because we had an incubator, we were given three precious eggs to try to hatch and raise. The owner agreed we could keep half of whatever hatched. We knew going in that this would be difficult given we had no experience, but with three great minds that are able to grab information and learn quickly, we agreed. Besides, we had built in support systems with the owner of the Peacocks.

The brilliant plumage and amazing temperament of these birds will inspire not only your appreciation for their beauty but also an appreciation for their unique characteristics.

Whilst many feel that peacocks are more of an exotic accessory for your home, they are actually a very companionable bird. They enjoy human company and while they are not as attentive as a dog, they will interact with the people who care for them.

The beauty, grace and benefits of owning and raising Peacocks will be explained throughout this book and it is with those words that I want to help you to take your first step towards owning a Peacock.

We jumped in and started scouring the Internet for information. There is some great information out there – but it is hunt and peck for good solid info that is useful in any situation.

One of your first decisions will be whether to locate your coop inside a fenced area or outside the fenced area. Alternatively, if you have enough land, you may want to build a large pen enclosure as is seen on many zoo or wildlife rescue websites. The extra space allows for a small tree or two. When the call from another friend came in asking us to buy and take over the care of their mature birds, we thought carefully and then gratefully paid for the birds after shoring up the largest pen we had. The structure is basically a car shed from Harbor Freight (about 200 bucks). That large structure built for our laying peahens became the home of the Peking duck and the two mature peafowl. After some modification we were now ready to bring home the birds.

Chapter 1. A brief Overview Of The Peacock

Short History of the Peacock

The peacock has been revered for thousands of years, and although the peacock has been found throughout the world as both domestic pets and in feral communities, the peacock is native to India and Burma. In fact, you can still see several species of peafowl in India and Burma.

Throughout history, the peacock has been admired for its plumage. It was imported into Egypt and while it is not clear how they were imported, many historians believe that the bird arrived in Egypt with the Phoenicians. From Egypt, peacocks spread throughout the Mediterranean. They have been linked to many ancient gods in several cultures including Ancient Greek Gods, Ancient Romans, and Hinduism.

By the 1300`s, peafowl were found throughout Europe and were a popular sign of wealth and sophistication. Many rich landowners and nobility had peacocks and peafowl on their properties.

This trend continued throughout history and the peacock became a status symbol throughout the world. It was domesticated partly for homes and also for zoos and it has also been adopted as a symbol for modern culture, television stations and religions.

Although the peacock has a long history with its native home, it was not officially accepted as the state bird of India until 1963. It is considered a sacred bird in India and is protected by the Indian law. In the rest of the world, the peacock and peafowl still make delightful pets that are as graceful as they are beautiful.

The thought of breeding and raising these exotic birds took over our imaginations and we quickly learned about the birds. The national bird of India is indeed a magnificent creation and is protected by law. For the backyard farmer, the differences between a peafowl and peahens or roosters are incredible.

1. The peafowl birds are considered cousins to the pheasant. They can fly high with power and are strong birds.

2. They are loud and can be heard at the neighbor's house a mile away. It is not unusual for them to travel a quarter mile to visit the neighbor's home.

3. They perceive loss of their flock members and will cry out if they are missing another peafowl. Even birds only one week old cry out. This cry of loss can be quite loud.

4. Eggs are not plentiful, and are limited to up to eight per season, but unlike peahens they can reproduce for up to 10 years.

After reaching maturity at about two years of age, the birds can reproduce and raise their peachicks without much human intervention. Males might not be mature until three years of age. The bird's normal lifespan is about 20 -23 years, but some captive birds can live much longer – into their 40s. That is amazing and may necessitate providing for their future through your last will and testament.

In our opinion so far, the peacocks are a bit easier to deal with than peahens and while they like their privacy they seem to tolerate their humans pretty well. They are excellent free rangers – although we have to protect ours from coyotes and such. Our peacocks love gobbling up scrap food and leftovers putting our peahens to shame.

All in all, you have made a great choice of exotic birds to keep in your backyard. There is so much you can do with raising peacocks and their beauty is calming to the soul that is rushed and stressed by life's pressures.

Chapter 2. Facts About The Peacock

Now that we have gone over the history of peafowl, it is time to cover some basic facts about the birds. Remember that many of these questions will be answered fully later on in this book, but for right now, I have provided you with some answers to the most pressing questions.

Are they good with children?
Generally, peafowl will ignore children but, as with all animals, you should not leave a child unattended with a peacock or peafowl. They may view the child as a threat and can be aggressive during nesting season.

Are they clean?
Although peacocks and peafowl are considered to be fairly clean, they are not recommended for apartments or for inside. They do require their own space like other livestock and will go to the washroom inside if they are brought in.

Can they live in cold climates?
Despite the fact that peacocks are a tropical bird whose natural habitat is a warm climate, they survive surprisingly well in colder climates. In fact, with proper shelter and care, peacocks and peafowl can live in climates that fall below 0 degrees in the winter.

Are they noisy?
The answer to this question is both yes and no. Many times during the year, peafowl are quiet and are a well-mannered bird, however, peacocks tend to become nosier during mating season.

Do Peacocks make good pets?
The answer to this question is both a yes and a no and it really depends on what type of pet you are looking for. If you are looking for one that dotes on you, then no, the peacock and peafowl are not for you. However, if you are looking for a charming companion that will alert you to strange things, then yes, they are excellent companions.

How big do peacocks and peahens get?

Although the train can be quite impressive on a peacock, in general, a peacock is usually 40 to 46 inches in length when fully grown, from beak to tail without the train, and they weigh about 8 to 14 pounds on average. The train itself usually grows an additional 78 to 90 inches. Peahens are slightly smaller and are usually 36 to 38 inches in length and weigh 6 to 9 pounds.

Lifespan of a peacock?

If you are looking for a short lived pet, then the peacock is not the proper pet for you. This bird tends to have a very long lifespan, with the bird living 15 to 20 years in the wild and up to 40 years in captivity, on average.

Are they difficult to care for?

Like all pets, peacocks and peafowl present their own challenges but if you have the proper housing and set up for the peafowl, then they are not usually difficult to care for.

How long do they take to mature?

Although a peacock or peafowl can reach their full size early, the peahens do not fully mature until 2 years. Peacocks do not mature fully until they are closer to 3 years old. At this time, the peacocks and peafowl can be used in a breeding program.

Temperament of the Peacock

Generally, peahens are a quiet and gentle bird. They are not usually over excitable and they tend to be very hardy birds. They do have a very innate grace and while they can be aggressive when they or their young are attacked, peahens tend to be very laid back birds.

It should be stressed that peacocks and peafowl are not domesticated in the true sense of the word. For this reason, you can expect many of the same behaviors of wild peacocks. They will nest and will often try to fly away. In addition, the peafowl will be wary of people approaching them; however, with proper luring and socialization, peafowl will come within a few feet of their owners to eat.

Any potential owner of peafowl should remember that this is not a bird you can carry around or pet.

Despite answering some of the basic questions in this chapter, it is important to look at all the aspects of raising, caring for and breeding your peacocks and peafowl.

Temperament of peacocks and peafowl can differ between species and subspecies; however, since the majority of domestic peafowl are Indian Blues, they generally have the same type of temperament.

When we look at the temperament of peafowl, it is important to look at the males separately from the females.

Peacocks, in turn, show many of the same personalities as the peahens. Usually, they do not have an agitated temperament but they can be quite protective. During mating season, they do become more aggressive and can become quite territorial.

The rest of the year, peacocks become very quiet and gentle birds that simply go about their day to day activities.

Chapter 3. Raising Peacocks As Pets

Before you purchase a peacock or any type of peafowl, it is important to ask yourself a few questions since peafowl have an exceptionally long life. These are not pets that you purchase for the short term as you can expect at least 20 years with your birds, if not longer.

Now that some of your questions about peacocks and peafowl have been answered, it is time to decide if you are ready to raise your own.

Remember, that any type of animal you bring into your home is going to take a large commitment from you and peafowl are no exception.

This is a bird that needs space as well as the proper set up in order for them to thrive, so it is important to have both of these before you even consider bringing a peacock home.

Do you rent or own?
If you rent a home, then you should avoid purchasing a peafowl, even if you rent a large farm. Unlike dogs and cats, peafowl are not animals that you can move into an apartment if you have to move to a new rental. Remember that this is a long term animal that needs a good sized backyard space.

Do you have the time?
Although peafowl are not as time consuming as other pets, you do need to have enough time to care for them properly. Keeping their bedding clean, making sure they stay on your property and feeding them take a daily commitment. If you cannot make that kind of commitment, then you should avoid purchasing your own peafowl.

Are you looking for an affectionate pet?
If the answer is yes, then the peacock is not the right pet for you. This is a semi domesticated animal so they do not usually get too close to their owners. Even ones that have been socialized enough to a handler will still

stay a few feet away and will not be a bird that likes to perch on their owner's shoulder or even be near their owner.

What type of dwelling do you live in?
Although peacocks and peafowl can do well in a smaller style of yard, homes with acreage are the better choice for these birds since they do enjoy roaming on their property. In addition, peacocks can be very noisy during mating season and this makes them less ideal for city dwellings. However, they have done well in communities that allow livestock such as peahens in backyards. They are not recommended for apartments and need a yard.

Can you provide the proper safety for your pet?
Lastly, providing the proper safety for your peafowl is very important since this bird can often fall victim to foxes and other predators. They will defend their young and nest; however, it is up to the breeder and owner to really make sure that the proper safety measures are in place for their peafowl to prevent them from being attacked and or injured.

One thing that should be pointed out is that a peacock cannot be made to fit into a lifestyle. These are birds that require space and proper care and you need to be willing and able to provide both.

Do you have access to an avian vet?
All animals, including peafowl, require regular medical care, so it is important to have an avian vet in your area. If you do not, then it may not be the ideal situation for your peafowl. Vets specializing in birds will understand the many challenges that owning a peacock can have and they will be able to help you maintain the best health for your birds.

Pros and Cons of Owning the peacock
Like every other type of animal, there are a number of pros and cons that you should consider before you purchase your own birds and I will go over both of them to help you make the best decision.

Pros of owning a peacock
Easy Care: Peafowl are very easy to care for and have many of the same needs that peahens have. Vaccinations are necessary, as is proper housing but they don't require a lot of extra care.

Profitable: If you are interested in breeding peafowl, you can actually make a fair amount of profit if you do it properly.

Beautiful: One of the biggest pros of owning and raising peafowl is that you have a beautiful animal to watch on a daily basis.

Inexpensive: While you can pay a large amount for some types of peafowl, the actual cost of care is quite low. Many do very well on inexpensive feed and outside of the start-up costs and vaccination costs; you won't have a large amount of upkeep costs.

Quiet: Generally, peafowl are quiet birds. There are periods of the season when they aren't but for most of the year you shouldn't have too much noise.

Guarding: No, they generally won't attack an intruder; however, most peafowl will make noise if something is unusual in the yard.

Generally, peafowl are an easy bird to raise and care for and the biggest advantage of owning a peafowl is simply the joy of watching the inquisitive birds in the yard.

Cons of owning a peacock

Predation: As I have mentioned, predation can be a problem with peafowl so you will need to be aware of this and also understand how to prevent it.

Dietary Needs: While peafowl are usually very easy to care for, dealing with their diet can be a bit overwhelming and can be costly if it is not done properly. Make sure you are aware of this before you purchase your peafowl.

Lifespan: The long lifespan of peafowl can be both a bonus and a negative.

Noise: While peafowl are fairly quiet during most of the year, during the breeding season, both peahens and peacocks can be quite noisy.

Ranging: If you are interested in having your peafowl range through your yard, you should be aware of the fact that they range quite far. In fact, they will often go miles away from home and this can put them at risk of predators or being injured on the highways.

Expensive Start Up: Like most animals, the start-up cost can be quite expensive when you take into account the different equipment you need, which I will go over later on in this book.

As with all animals, it is important to understand both the challenges and advantages of owning and raising peafowl. Owning them can be wonderful but it is a commitment and shouldn't be entered into lightly.

Free Range or Penned

The last thing that you should consider before you even go to purchase your peafowl is whether you would like to have them free range or whether you want to pen them.

Although it may seem like a simple choice, it isn't. Free ranging peafowl can be wonderful but they can also be very challenging. In addition, penned peafowl can be challenging as well.

What is Free Ranging?

Free ranging your peafowl is when you are able to have the peafowl move around your property without being hindered by pens or fences. Generally, free ranging peafowl become wilder than your penned peafowl and they often forage for themselves, which can cut down on the amount of work involved with feeding them.

What are the Benefits of Free Ranging?

Pros for free ranging your birds can include:

Less Time: Ranging peafowl require less of your time and you can simply set up one area for feeding and watering your birds. They will take care of the rest.

Less Space: When you first bring your birds home, you will need to have space for your aviary, which I will go over later in this book, but afterwards, the birds don't need a very large set space. This can save time, money and space in your yard.

Amazing to watch: Let's face it, the main reason that people purchase peafowl is for the beautiful train of the peacock. Having the birds free range will give you more opportunity to see it and will also give you the chance to watch the birds explore and interact with the world around them.

Easier Care: Since they are free ranging and taking care of themselves, it can be quite easy to care for the birds. In addition, you don't have to clean out any pens when your birds free range.

Less Cost: Generally, the cost of caring for a free range peafowl is lower, especially when you look at feeding as the peafowl finds much of its own food.

As you can see, there are many benefits to having your birds free range and it really depends on what you want.

What are the Disadvantages of Free Ranging?
Cons for free ranging your birds can include:

Indiscriminate Breeding: Lastly, when peafowl free range, it can be harder to make your own breeding program to ensure that you get exactly what you want from a pairing.

High Predation Rate: Although penned peafowl can fall prey to predators, those that free range are at a higher risk from predators. Most predation occurs when the peahens are nesting or have chicks.

High Risk of Injury: Since peafowl will range quite far when they are out, they can be more susceptible to injury from roads, people and from eating things that can be harmful to them. This can result in higher vet costs for you or even in the loss or your peafowl.

Can disappear: Free range peafowl can disappear from your property, especially when they are first released. Although people don't realize it, peafowl can fly quite well and can also hop upwards over 30 feet. They will easily jump a 6 foot fence and disappear.

Destructive: Free ranging peafowl can be very destructive to a yard and they will eat plants and many other items in your garden if they are allowed to range.

In the end, the main difference between free ranging and penning your birds is simply the risks involved for your birds. The more they range, the harder it can be to keep them safe, however, having them in the pen can mean it is more difficult to enjoy them to their fullest.

Chapter 4. Choosing The Right Peacock To Raise

In this chapter, I will cover aspects of choosing the right type of Peacock as well as what to look for in your peafowl breeder and how to sex your birds. If you find that you are ready for a peacock, it is now time to start looking for the peafowl that you want to have. Although you may not be aware of it, there are over 180 different varieties of peafowl and it can make choosing the right one quite difficult.

Types of Peacocks

Although we often think of peacocks when we think of peafowl, there are actually many different varieties and it is important to be aware of them. Most peafowl are raised in the same manner; however, there are some slight differences in some of them.

Peafowl come in several different types with a number of varieties in each subspecies. There are two species of peafowl, which are known as the Pavo Cristatus and the Pavo Muticus and one hybrid species of peafowl, known as the Spalding.

Indo-Chinese Green

Another subspecies of the green peafowl, the Indo Chinese Green are a brilliant green bird that is found both in the wild and in captivity. They are a very rare peafowl to have and only a handful of breeders carry this species.

Ease of Raising: Medium.
Origin: Indochina, Eastern Burma and Siam.
Coloration: Peacock: Light blue and yellow skin on the face, the body is bluish green with a dark green underside. The neck and head are metallic green. Very similar in colour to the Java Green, however, they are slightly muted in colour.

Peahen: Similar coloration to the male Java Green, and can often be mistaken for the other green peafowl. They have muted colours and the Indo Chinese Green has a buff border around the breast.
Peachick: Dark greyish-brown in colour.

Pavo Cristatus
Also known as the Indian Blue Peafowl, Blue Peafowl or India Peafowl, this is the more common of the peacock species.
While there are patterns in the Indian Blue Peafowl, the main snapshot of the bird is as follows:

Indian Blue
As I have mentioned many times, Indian Blues are the more common peacock found in zoos and on farms. These are the birds that are usually depicted in art.
Ease of Raising: Very Easy, good for new breeders.
Origin: India, Burma and Malaya.
Coloration: Peacock: Blue chest, neck and head with white and black striped shoulders and hints of green and gold feathers throughout the bird. The long tail has a large eye or crescent pattern.
Peahen: Brown in colour, the Indian Blue peahen also have iridescent green on their neck as well as a white belly.
Peachick: Greyish-brown in colour.

Pavo Muticus
Also known as the Green Peafowl, and there are three subspecies of green peafowl. Green peafowl are not as common as Indian Blue Peafowl, but they are slowly gaining some popularity with breeders. Green peafowl tend to be slightly taller and leaner than blue peafowl. The subspecies of green peafowl are:

Burmese Green
Some varieties of peafowl have been created through cross breeding; however, the Burmese Green is a wild peafowl. They are actually quite rare in captivity and even rarer in the wild. They are an endangered species and while they look similar to an Indian Blue, they have a muted colouring.

Ease of Raising: Medium.

Origin: Burma.

Coloration: Peacock: Dull blue and green in colour with a dark blue throat and blue back. Wing coverts are black.

Peahen: Blue coloration with muted brown and black feathers over their entire body.

Peachick: Greyish-brown in colour.

Java Green

Also known as the Javanese peafowl, the Java Green is another green peafowl that can be found in the wild as well as in captivity. Again, this bird is endangered; however, they are the most common green peafowl in captivity.

Ease of Raising: Medium.

Origin: Java and Malay Peninsula.

Coloration: Peacock: Light blue and yellow skin on the face, the body is bluish green with a dark green underside. The neck and head are metallic green.

Peahen: Similar coloration to the male Java Green, the peahen has muted colours and dark barring on the tail.

Peachick: Dark greyish-brown in colour.

Spalding

The Spalding was developed by crossing the Green Peafowl with the Indian Blue Peafowl. They are usually lighter than other peafowl and are quickly gaining popularity. The snapshot of the Spalding is:

Ease of Raising: Easy.

Origin: California, United States.

Coloration: Peacock: Bluish Green chest, neck and head with white and black striped shoulders and hints of green and gold feathers throughout the bird. There is usually a patch of yellow on the head and the crest is usually shorter than either the Indian Blue or the Green Peafowl. The long tail has a large eye or crescent pattern.

Peahen: Similar coloration to other peahens, there is a greenish blue feathering on the neck and chest with a small yellow patch on the face.

Peachick: Dark greyish-brown in colour.

Patterns

Generally, when you are looking at the different varieties of peafowl that you can choose from, you are actually looking at the patterns of the feathers. There are many different feather patterns; however, they are grouped into the following categories:

Pied

Pied is found in many of the peafowl species and is a colour mutation where the feathers are splotched with white. The mutation is caused by an incomplete dominant gene and you can breed pied from pied birds or by crossing other patterns, although they do not breed true.

Generally, the white can take up a small amount of the feathers or it can take upwards of 60% of the bird. Even the train can have splotches and patches of white. A common snapshot of the pied colouring can be seen in the Indian Blue Pied.

Indian Blue Pied

A pied peafowl is an interesting bird, as it has the colouring of an Indian Blue but will be splotched with white. The pied pattern occurs due to an incomplete dominant gene and it is important to note that the chicks are not always pied. In fact, 25% of the offspring can be born white.

Ease of Raising: Easy.

Origin: India.

Coloration: Peacock: Blue chest, neck and head with white and completely black shoulders and hints of green and gold feathers throughout the bird. The long tail has a large eye or crescent pattern. The entire bird is covered with splotches and patches of white and some have white on their train. Peahen: Brown in colour, the peahen also has iridescent green on their neck as well as a white belly. Again, the peahen can be covered in white splotches.

Choosing Your Peacock

Generally, I recommend that all new enthusiasts start with adults, although you can start with young adults. Chicks can be a bit more difficult to raise, since they need some special diets; such as starter feeds and they do require the care and protection of their mother peahen. At this point, you may realize that there are a lot of different peafowl and it can be a bit overwhelming when you are trying to decide on your own peafowl.

Although everyone has a favourite peafowl, I always recommend that new enthusiasts take the time to research each of the varieties. The main point that you should look at is what type of colour you are interested in before you actually start narrowing down the birds you want to bring in.

When you have narrowed it down to a colour or species that you want, then it is time to decide between adults and chicks.

Some of the benefits of starting with a chick are:

Enjoyment: Watching the peafowl grow can be just as entertaining and delightful as watching the full-grown peafowl.

Less Noise: Because peafowl do not reach maturity until they are roughly 2 years of age, there is a longer period of time without any loud noises.

Can socialize them your own way: While they will never be completely tame, some breeders have found that handling chicks when they are young can encourage a stronger bond between bird and owner.

Cons of purchasing chicks are:

Is the breeder part of the NPIP? NPIP means the National Poultry Improvement Program and it is designed to prevent diseases and the spread of diseases in birds, namely poultry. Breeders who are NPIP approved work hard to ensure that the birds they are breeding and raising are free of disease. Starting with an NPIP approved bird will help ensure that your peafowls are healthy.

Although you can purchase only one peafowl, it is often better for both the bird and you to purchase a breeding pair, or male and female. This ensures that you have the ability to produce your own young and you will have double the enjoyment with your birds. More work: Chicks require a bit more care than an adult peafowl and you will need a better set up so the chicks stay warm.

Difficult to Sex: Some peafowl can be sexed, where you determine the gender, very easily while others can be very difficult. In some cases, such as whites, it can take over 2 years to determine if the peafowl is male or female.

Longer Wait: Most males do not begin to have a train until they are over 2 years of age and some may not have a full train until they are 5 years of age. Starting with a chick means that it will be that much longer before you can enjoy the beauty of the peacock.

With adult peafowl, you will have to make do with the temperament that the breeder established. If the birds were left on their own a lot, you may find that they are a bit more skittish with humans than ones that have been socialized.

When you are choosing peafowl, take your time choosing your breeder. Here are a few points with the breeder that you should consider:

• How long has the breeder been raising peafowl? Although you can go with a newly established breeder, it is better to go with one that has been established for a long time. These breeders often become a resource for you and will help you set up your space.

• Is the breeder open to discuss peafowl? If the breeder is just trying to sell you the peafowl, then you should probably look elsewhere. As I have already mentioned, you really want a peafowl breeder who will answer the questions you have.

• Is the facility clean? It may be more difficult to gauge the facility if the peafowl are free to roam, but you should make sure that the nesting areas are clean and that there isn't a lot of filth where the birds are. In addition, make sure that there is no overcrowding in any pens that are set up.

• Are the birds healthy? Make sure that all the birds you see are healthy. Ask about their worming schedule, when the last time the birds were wormed and what they do to oversee the health of the birds. If you find that the birds look underweight or their feathers are dull, then you should look elsewhere for your bird.

- One thing that you should always check is the overall health of your birds. Make sure that the birds have the majority of their feathers, unless it is moulting season, and also make sure that the colouring is right. If you have a bird that is known for having iridescence on the feathers, you will want to make sure that the feathers are iridescent.

- In addition, look for birds that have an alert and curious look to them. The neck should be long and strong and a healthy peafowl will hold its head up. Eyes should be clear of any lumps or discoloration and the bird should have an alert look in the eye.

- Plumage should be full and the overall shape of the bird should be strong and thick. Overall, the breast should be very thick. Although most people don't look for it, toes should be straight and it is important to make sure that the beak is straight as well.

- When you are looking for peafowl, the best rule of thumb is to really go with your gut instinct. If something seems off, then find a different breeder and remember that you do not have to go with the first breeder you find.

Chapter 5. Bringing Your Peacock Home

Bringing your peafowl home properly will ensure that your peafowl have a long and happy life. Well, you have done it. You have chosen your bird and you are getting ready to bring it home. Before you do, however, there are a number of things that you should do, such as setting up pens.

Golden guidelines for introducing new peacocks to your flock

• Quarantine new birds.

• Introduce newcomers into the coop at night.

• Never add bantams or very young birds to established flocks of large adult poultry.

• Don't submit just one bird at a time!

• If blood is drawn, remove the victim to safety.

• Remove persistent bullies for a week or so, then reintroduce.

• Make sure extra sources of food and water are supplied to avoid established birds hogging it all.

• Be aware hens can go off lay for a while when introduced or when dealing with newcomers.

• Keep a very watchful eye over your newly expanded flock for any problems that might arise.

• Do your research. Some breeds should never be held together, and peacocks rarely play nice with other peacocks. People often start out with two or three peacocks but go on to add more birds to their flocks over time.

There are consequences to doing this. Fights are inevitable, although things usually settle down within a week or two.

Pens and Housing

No matter what you choose, I recommend that you build a laneway from all of your pens. The laneway should have a fully enclosed roof, either with wire or in a building, and should be about 8 feet wide and run past all the doors of each pen you have.

The doors of the pens should open fully into the laneway and there should be a door at the end of the laneway for you to access or to send the birds out of. The main reason for this laneway is so that you have added security if a bird runs out of a pen when you enter it.

Before you bring your peafowl home, it is important to set up your equipment and housing. Although you may be planning on conditioning your birds, you will need to have pens to keep the birds safe during the night.

The number of pens can vary, depending on the number of birds that you get, but in general, I recommend that you keep only two birds in each pen so that you don't have a lot of overcrowding.

When you are making a pen, you should consider a few factors. First, you will need an enclosed space where the birds can get out of the cold. You can either make a door for the birds to go in and out of, or you can just make a sheltered section in an outdoor enclosure.

In addition, it makes sorting much easier and you can simply herd the bird out of a pen and into a different pen. This reduces the amount of stress the birds feel as you will not have to capture the birds.

The pens themselves should consist of an inside stall, usually kept in a barn and the outdoor flight pen. The inside stall should be about 8 feet wide by 8 feet deep. The height should be also about 8 feet and there should be a wooden or wire roof to prevent the birds from flying up.

From the stall, there should be a small door for the birds to access the flight pen. The flight pens should also be 8 feet wide and 8 feet high but the length should be 42 feet long. This may seem like a huge space but, trust me, the birds will be much happier because of it.

Try to place flight pens on the south facing wall, as this usually provides them with more depth. Cover the first 10 feet of the flight pen with wood or metal to provide the birds with shade and shelter from rain.

The remaining part of the flight pen should be wire and you should never leave them uncovered. An 8-foot fence is nothing to a peafowl and they can easily jump them.
The wire I recommend that you use for the pens should be a 1 x 2-inch wire and if you can, I recommend that you place 1 inch knotted mesh over the tops of the flight pen, as the birds have been known to break through the covers.

When it comes to the environment in the pen, try to grow grass in the majority of the flight pen. If you are unable to, keep the dirt clean and free of debris; especially man-made debris, as peafowl will swallow it.

Next, keep a dirt area under the covered portion of the flight pen and also add a small amount of hay or straw. In the stall, cover the floor with hay or straw.

Special Permits
Most areas require you to have a clean bill of health on the birds you bring in. This keeps them from spreading diseases into the area, so a transport certificate will need to be cleared with both the Ministry of Agriculture and a local vet.

Once the birds are at your home, you should keep them in quarantine for the time that you are conditioning them to your property to ensure that there is no underlying illness that was overlooked.

In general, peafowl do not need any type of special permits to be owned. They are often classified as poultry so they only require the proper zoning laws appropriate to poultry.

One thing that I should mention, is that in most places, there are no special permits needed. However, as they fall under the category of agriculture animals, you need to make sure that you are allowed to have them in your area. Some cities and towns allow backyard poultry but others don't. Take the time before you purchase a peafowl to make sure that you are allowed to have them in your area.

Building a Roost
Roosts can be both heated and non-heated but generally, you should avoid using heated if you live in warm climates. If you live in a cold climate, then a few heated roosts can help keep temperatures bearable for the birds. In the pen and stall, make sure you have an area for the birds to roost. Roosts should be installed about 4 feet off of the ground, so the bird can easily get up without hitting the ceiling of the pen.

A heated roost is very easy to make. Run a strip of electric heat tape, which is used on water pipes, down the length of a 2 x 6 board twice. You want to leave 6 inches on either side of the roost.

Next, secure the tape with staples and hang the thermostat in a way so you can read the temperature easily.

Wrap the roost with thick carpet and leave a 4-inch space on either end of the board that is not lined with carpet.

Install the roost in the pen and if you need to, reinforce it with a second board to keep it from bowing.

Protection from Predators
For birds that are in a pen, constantly check the pen to make sure that the wire has not been disturbed. In addition, bury the 1 x 2-inch wire underground about 2 feet to prevent burrowing predators from getting at your birds.

For ones that will try to climb up and chew the pen, you can place an electric fence part way up the pen. This will deter any larger predators as well.

If your peafowl are free ranging, there is not a lot that you can do to protect them from predators. I recommend that you keep them in an enclosure during the night but if you can't, then you should allow the trees in your yard to have branches of about 10 feet above the ground.

Thin out the trees a bit for better roosting but not too much, as the birds will not feel protected. Have enough roosting spots in your yard so the birds can see the space around them clearly.

Bringing the Peacock home

When the peafowl arrive home, place the container into the pen and place some food outside near the container. Carefully open the container and remove the tail wrappings from the bird. Do not rush and try to remain calm so you don't worry the bird.

Once the tail wrapping is off, step back and allow the peafowl to move out of the container on his own. Don't rush the bird at all.

When the bird is out exploring the pen on his own, remove the container and then leave the bird alone.
During those first few days, try to keep the peafowl inside the stall and minimize the amount of contact you have with it. Feed and water the peafowl but simply coexist with it. Don't try to touch the bird or get too close unless there seems to be an illness occurring.

Now that you have your pen and roosting set up for your peafowl, it is time to bring the peafowl home. One point that I should mention is that you should purchase your peafowl from a breeder near you.

While birds can adjust to different climates, finding birds from a breeder in your area will help prevent any problems from a climate change.
Bring the birds home in a secure peafowl container and try to make the trip as uneventful as possible. Don't fuss with the birds during transport and keep them in the back of an enclosed vehicle. Do not transport them in the back of a pickup truck as this can cause stress for the birds.

After a few days, you can begin to socialize with the bird a bit more but those first few days should be quiet, calm and free of a lot of outside stimulation.

By bringing your peafowl home properly, you are sure to have more success with your birds.

Chapter 6. Taking Care Of Your Peacock

In fact, outside of a proper diet, peafowl will deal with preening their feathers and can often go off on their own for longer periods of time, only checking in for their regular meal.

That being said, there are still some things that you should do to maintain the overall health of your bird. I will discuss feeding your peafowl in the next chapter, but in this chapter, I will go over the daily and yearly care involved in keeping your peafowl healthy.

Although there is a lot of information throughout this book, caring for a peacock or any peafowl is really not that difficult. Peafowl do not require a lot of extra care and while you can spend a lot of time watching the birds, many take care of their own needs on a day-to-day basis.

Daily Care

Examine the bird on a daily basis. Check to make sure that there are no unusual signs of illness and that your birds are alert and curious. If there is any listless behaviour or the birds seem off in either appearance or temperament, then it is important to bring the birds in to see a veterinarian. As I have mentioned, you don't have to be as involved in daily care as you need to be with some other animals. It is important that you provide your peafowl with daily food, especially if they are penned, but I will go over feeding in the following chapter.

Since most peafowl remain rather wary of their owners, it can be a bit difficult and unsettling for the bird to capture it each day for an examination, so I recommend that you merely carry out a visual examination. If you see something that makes you nervous, capture the bird and then do a physical examination before contacting your vet.

With feed, place the grain mixture into an automatic feeder and mount it about 8 to 24 inches off the ground so the birds have easy access to it. The remainder of the food, including the treats, can be placed on the ground or in pans on the ground. Like many other types of birds, peafowl like to scratch for the food so providing them with an opportunity to do so will also help avoid your birds becoming bored.

If your peafowl are free ranging, then you can keep cleaning the pens to a minimum and will only have to clean the pens when the birds are using it. I recommend that you keep a few pens available to your birds so they have somewhere to roost and also so you have somewhere for the birds if they are sick.

Once you have given your birds the daily visual examination, feed them. Peafowl should be fed twice per day, once in the early morning just after dawn and once in the early evening, just before sunset.

During the rest of the day, you can have a few treats for the birds but they will do most of their feeding during the start and the end of the day. Water should be left out throughout the day and I should mention a few things about feeders and waterers. Firstly, you should never place your water in a drip style container that hangs above the bird. This can cause a lot of problems and affect the health of your bird.

Instead, use a bucket or pan where the water can rest on the ground. Make sure the container is not too large or you will find that your peafowl prefer to stand in the water instead of drink it.

If the peafowl are kept in pens, try to tidy the pens on a daily basis and give it a good cleaning about once a week. Keep bedding clean. One interesting fact to point out is that peafowl often "drop their droppings" when they are preening themselves and many have a preening site where they like to sit. Simply spray this area down once a day to keep the amount of bird droppings to a minimum.

The rest of the time, just remove feathers, which you can keep for decoration and also rake the dirt of the pen to keep the area clean and fresh. Place in straw for bedding to keep your peafowl comfortable.

And that is really all you need to do with the general care. Peafowl don't need to be bathed on a regular basis and will keep their feathers clean on their own.

Clipping the Wing

If you decide to clip your bird's wings, you should be prepared to clip the wings every few months, usually every 2 to 3 months depending on individual bird and also on how short you cut the wing.

Before you decide to clip the wings of your peafowl, it is important to really make sure that it needs to be done. Birds use their wings for escape and while they can jump quite high, not being able to fly away for safety can leave them at risk of predation.

In addition, clipping is viewed as cruel by many in the peafowl world and some breeders may have specific recommendations regarding clipping their young birds.

To trim the wings, follow these steps:

1. Make sure the bird is safe and won't get hurt. It is better to work with the bird on the ground.

2. Hold both of the legs and have an assistant stretch out the wing.

3. With sharp scissors, begin cutting the wing. The best way to do this is to follow the tertiary feathers, which are the inner flight feathers, as a guide.

4. Cut one feather at a time, following the tertiary feathers.

5. Clip until all the feathers on one wing are trimmed.

With peafowl, you should only clip one wing on the bird to prevent your birds from flying away. Once they are clipped, release the bird safely and then clip the next bird's wing.

Health Concerns

When choosing a veterinarian, look for a vet that has experience with peafowl. A vet should take into consideration the differences between exotic peafowl and other types of poultry.

Worms

ALL BIRDS GET WORMS, whether caged or free. Keep your birds de-wormed. Some swear that you can do this naturally by daily dosing with

Diatomaceous Earth, Cayenne Pepper and/or Garlic. Others will use ground up pumpkin seed and a diet that is toxic to worms. Most owners would not risk their birds' lives and use chemical de-wormers.

The standard is to deworm with a chemical wormer 2x a year. Wormer is best administered in the water, as birds may not eat enough of the wormer feed to kill all the parasites. Some owners prefer to use paste wormers and disguise it in the bird's favorite bread, watching carefully to make sure it is all ingested. Some force feed the wormer, or inject it under the skin. The application is usually repeated after 10 days (read your directions) to kill any hatched eggs.

Consult your vet at least once or read the recommendations on the literature enclosed.
Some things to know:
Safe-guard, aka Panacor, is used widely and can be administered in water.
Valbazen in a suspension formula is a wormer that can be administered in water.

Ivomec is a wormer that kills most external parasites as well as internal worms and is easily used even though the birds may have to be handled to administer the drug.

Fenbendezol is another vet recommended wormer.

Another type of wormer is CORID and is used for coccidiosis in peafowl. Symptoms include diarrhea in birds. The medicine is administered over the course of 4-5 days and is not repeated.

Most experts advise alternating the wormers to avoid resistance to any one type of wormer. After worming –treat the pen by cleaning thoroughly.

Miscellaneous health concerns
Keeping your birds healthy will depend on their housing, diet and stress levels. It can be puzzling to find out why your bird seems "off." Finding a vet is a great idea. You can also look online for vet consultants for peacocks. .

Having a peahen with a stuck egg (egg binding) can be traumatic and the answer advised could be as easy as adding ground calcium to the diet or advise giving a 20 minute warm bath (right catch the peahen for that) or even applying KY jelly to the vent. Make sure you locate a vet familiar with peacocks and keep the office number on hand.

Mites and Lice

Mites can be treated with Scalex Mite spray, Avian Insect Liquidator or Scatt (moxidectine). DE (Diatomaceous Earth) can be used to dust the birds for both mites and lice. Keeping a dust bath area open for your birds is important to prevent infestations. Cleaning roosts and nesting boxes and treating the bedding is important. Spray a mite/lice killer into all the cracks of the nesting area and housing.

Make sure to wash your clothes immediately (changing outdoors if possible) as the mites can spread to humans.

Recognizing Mites: some mites are visible and the symptoms are easy to spot: Restlessness or listlessness, preening, sometimes feathers will be missing and bald spots occur. Birds may avoid going into their nesting house. You can check the house for the little red buggers.

Lice can be seen when feathers are pulled apart – eggs are usually laid near the vent area of the birds and are attached to the feather shaft.

Wormers and Vaccinations

It is important to have them vaccinated on a regular basis. Check with your vet to find out what diseases have been prevalent in the area so you are vaccinating against the right strains. At the end of this chapter, I have listed a number of diseases that your peafowl can be affected by and have indicated the ones where vaccinations can work as preventative care.

Administering Oral Medication

If you are worming your birds or have run into a situation where you need to administer oral medication, it is important to know how to properly administer it. If you do not administer the medication properly, you could risk your bird drowning in the medication or not receiving the proper amount.

To administer oral medication, follow these steps:

1. Fill a syringe (one that does not have a needle but has a very long and fine end) with the medication.

2. Insert the syringe in the mouth and push it down slightly so that it is just past the trachea opening. Be very careful when you do this to prevent injury.

3. Slowly press the plunger down.

4. Once the medication has been administered, remove the syringe from the bird's mouth. Let the bird open and close his mouth several times and watch him to make sure that the bird does not have any negative side effects from the medication.

5. After a few minutes, let the bird go.

6. Catch the peafowl and have someone help you. Make sure the bird is held securely for both your safety and its own. It is better to work with the bird on the ground and hold onto both of the legs.

7. Once the bird is secure, carefully open the bird's mouth.

8. Have your assistant hold the top of the beak and place his fingers between the two parts of the beak to keep it opened for you to work.

9. Look inside the mouth. You will notice that there is a trachea tube at the base of the tongue. Make sure that you do not put the medication near that tube.

When it comes to illnesses, most breeders agree that peafowl are fairly healthy; however, this does not mean that they never get sick. It is important to be aware of the diseases that can affect the overall health of your birds to ensure that your peafowl remains healthy.

Viruses

Like all animals, peafowl are susceptible to some viruses. Some can be medicated while others cannot and will simply need to be treated.

Sinusitis

Symptoms: Sinuses in the eye swell.
Cause: Transmitted between hen and unborn chicks.
Treatment: No cure but antibiotics are used to treat the symptoms. All birds with Sinusitis are lifelong carriers and should not be bred.
Vaccination: No

Hemorrhagic Enteritis

Symptoms: Inflammation of the intestines, haemorrhaging in the intestines. High mortality rate. Usually affects birds between 4 to 13 weeks.
Cause: Transmitted between birds through faecal droppings.
Treatment: Antibiotics are used to treat the secondary infections caused by the disease but there is no treatment for the disease itself. Clean pens and feed will help prevent the spread.
Vaccination: Yes, yearly vaccination can prevent the disease. Clean pens and sound husbandry will also prevent it.

Fowl Pox

Symptoms: Lesions on the skin, raised, crater like scars, conjunctiva in the eye.
Cause: Transmitted through the bite of mosquitoes infect with the virus.
Treatment: Topical creams for the lesions
Vaccination: Yes, can be administered before and during outbreak.

Newcastle Disease

Symptoms: Respiratory distress possibly resulting in death
Cause: Transmitted between birds.
Treatment: No treatment. The illness runs for 14 days. Vaccination has been successful at controlling the disease.
Vaccination: Yes, should be administered yearly.

M. synoviae

Symptoms: Inflamed joints, arthritis.
Cause: Transmitted between hen and unborn chicks.
Treatment: No cure but antibiotics are used to treat the symptoms. All birds with M. synoviae are lifelong carriers and should not be bred.
Vaccination: No

Air Sacculitis

Symptoms: Inflamed air sacs and air reservoirs, excretion of pus from affected area.

Cause: Transmitted between hen and unborn chicks.

Treatment: No cure but antibiotics are used to treat the symptoms. All birds with Air Sacculitis are lifelong carriers and should not be bred.

Vaccination: No

Bacteria

There are actually a number of bacteria that can be spread between birds, which can be very serious for your peafowl. In addition, some of the bacterial diseases can be spread between bird species so it is important to treat any diseases immediately.

Vaccination: No

Arizona Infection

Symptoms: Loss of appetite, dead eggs or chicks shortly after hatching, and diarrhoea. High mortality rate.

Cause: Caused by the Arizona bacterium. Spread from parent birds to unhatched chicks.

Treatment: Neomycin and/or nitrofuran are used to treat and control the disease.

Vaccination: No

Avian Tuberculosis

Symptoms: Weight loss, decrease in egg production, diarrhoea, and increased thirst. Usually affects birds between the age of 3 and 4 years old.

Cause: Caused by the bacteria Mycobacterium avian. Spread from bird to bird through poor sanitation.

Treatment: No treatment. Prevention is done through proper sanitation and management of the aviary.

Vaccination: No

Fowl Typhoid

Symptoms: Loss of appetite, dead eggs or chicks shortly after hatching, diarrhoea, drooping wings, and dehydration. Death of the bird.

Cause: Caused by the bacteria Salmonella gallinarum. Spread from parent birds to unhatched chicks.
Treatment: No cure, all birds that have been identified as having fowl typhoid are destroyed. Birds with the disease should not be bred.
Vaccination: No

Pullorum

Symptoms: Loss of appetite, dead eggs or chicks shortly after hatching, diarrhoea, drooping wings, and dehydration. Death of the bird.
Cause: Caused by the bacteria Salmonella pullorum. Spread from parent birds to unhatched chicks.
Treatment: No cure, all birds that have been identified as having fowl typhoid are destroyed. Birds with the disease should not be bred.

Paratyphoid

Symptoms: Trembling, diarrhoea, blindness, loss of appetite, weakness. Usually affects young chicks between the ages of 8 to 28 days and can result in death of the bird.
Cause: Caused by over 2000 serotypes of Salmonella bacteria. Spread from parent birds to chicks through the egg.
Treatment: Neomycin and/or nitrofuran are used to treat and control the disease
Vaccination: No

Fowl Cholera

Symptoms: Haemorrhaging, high mortality rate.
Cause: Caused by the bacteria Pasteurella multocida. Spread from bird to bird through poor sanitation.
Treatment: Treatment through sulfa drugs and antibiotics.
Decontamination of the flock as well as the equipment and aviary needs to be done to prevent further infections.
Vaccination: Yes but not completely successful at preventing the disease.

Mycoplasma

Mycoplasma Galli-septic um is a particularly nasty bacterial infection that causes chronic respiratory disease (CRD) and infectious sinusitis in peacocks and many other birds, including turkeys and pigeons. Symptoms include difficulty with breathing, coughing, sneezing, a nasty nasal discharge and bubbly eyes. Don't mistake it for a cold. It's much more severe. If left untreated, mycoplasma can kill.

Symptoms

Mycoplasma may appear to be a cold at first. Peacocks do get colds, just like we do, but you'll know it's mycoplasma you're dealing with when the cold doesn't go away, and your birds exhibit the symptoms mentioned above.

If you suspect you have a mycoplasma outbreak in your flock, you can confirm it by heading down to the coop at night, when your peacocks are asleep, and just listen. Mycoplasma causes the air sacs and respiratory passages to produce sounds you'd expect to hear coming from the chest of an old man who smoked 20 a day for most of his adult life. It's a distressing noise to hear.

If it's at an advanced stage, infected birds will display bluish wattles and combs, meaning they aren't getting enough oxygen in their blood. A peacock in this condition is unlikely to last for much longer.

Individual responses to mycoplasma infection vary. Some birds die. Others show symptoms but recover. Some show no sign of being ill at all. As a matter of routine, you should quarantine all new birds before introducing them to your flock. Newcomers are likely to become infected within days if any of your established birds already have mycoplasma, even though they might not be showing signs of it.

Causes

Mycoplasma is an opportunistic infection that takes advantage of birds with immune systems already compromised by other diseases or stress. Events that might stress your birds out are sometimes unavoidable and nearly always commonplace. They include moving your peacocks into a new coop, adding new birds to your flock, changing their diet, changes in the weather and parasites.

Free-range peacocks that are not kept under cover are also susceptible to mycoplasma brought in by wild birds.

Diagnosis

A vet can run a blood test if you aren't sure if your flock has been infected with mycoplasma. Samples are sent away to be analyzed, so you could be waiting a few days for the results to come back.

Be advised that in some countries (not in the UK, though) mycoplasma is classified in law as a notifiable disease; this can mean all birds testing positive have to be culled. Therefore, in countries where this applies, such as the Republic of Ireland, poultry-keepers are well advised to have new stock tested for mycoplasma before confirming their purchase. It could save a lot of heartbreak and money.

Treatment

It's impossible to get rid of mycoplasma unless you have all your birds killed and you start over, having sterilized the ground and housing. Although the bacterium cannot survive for long outside a host, you would be advised to leave everything unused for a few weeks before restocking. Commercial poultry farmers cull all birds, infected or not when the presence of mycoplasma is confirmed. If treated quickly, though, mycoplasma need not be an automatic death sentence for a domestic flock.

Eggs produced by infected birds are perfectly okay to eat, although any that are laid during a course of treatment with medication is classed as unfit for human consumption and must be destroyed.

Tylan and Baytril are prescribed to treat mycoplasma, as they are broad-spectrum antibiotics. A course is typically administered for three to five days; at least one member of your flock will need to be seen by a vet before a prescription can be provided.

Chicks can be vaccinated against mycoplasma but adults cannot. It's difficult for home peacock-keepers to go down the vaccination route, though, because treatment can be expensive; vaccines are sold in quantities suitable for commercial flocks, where birds number in the thousands.

Prevention

The only way to avoid the risk of mycoplasma infection from wild birds is to keep your birds under cover at all times, which is frankly unrealistic and unappealing to most of those who keep peacocks at home.

Lice

Symptoms: Itching, restlessness, over preening

Cause: Lice are a small external parasite that eat skin, scales and feather debris. Spread from bird to bird and more commonly seen in peafowl that roam.

Treatment: Treatment with a pesticide. Make sure that treatment is bird safe.

Vaccination: No, treatment is the only way to deal with lice.

Chiggers

Symptoms: Scabby lesions on the thighs, breast, vent and undersides of the wings.

Cause: Common mite that is found in the environment.

Treatment: Usually no treatment for the mite, which falls off after 14 days of feeding, however, the lesions are treated with medication.

Vaccination: No

Ascaridia Worms

Symptoms: Intestinal distress, diarrhoea, depressed state due to blood loss

Cause: A worm that moves through the intestinal tract of the peafowl. Spread through the environment and through faeces.

Treatment: Treatment is done with piperazine worm medicine.

Vaccination: No, de-worming twice a year can help prevent.

Cecal Worms

Symptoms: Very few symptoms

Cause: Worms are spread from bird-to-bird. The cecal worm lives in the ceca of the peafowl.

Treatment: Treatment is done through wormers.

Vaccination: No, de-worming twice a year can help prevent.

Staphylococcus

Symptoms: Arthritis, septicema

Cause: Caused by the bacteria Staphylococcus aureus through poor sanitation in the environment.
Treatment: Treatment through antibiotics. Decontamination of the equipment and aviary needs to be done to prevent further infections.
Vaccination: No

Parasites

In addition to viruses and bacteria, peafowl and many other birds can become susceptible to various parasites. They can contract them from the environment or the parasites can be spread between birds.

In most cases, proper care and cleanliness of the aviary will help to prevent most of the parasites. For some, worming medications and treatments will help prevent and correct the problem.

Tapeworms
Symptoms: Weight loss, fragments of tapeworm in the faeces.
Cause: Spread through insects, crustaceans and arthropods, peafowl become infected by feeding from infected food.
Treatment: Treatment is done with worming medication.
Vaccination: No, de-worming twice a year can help prevent.

Capillaria Worms
Symptoms: Rough feathers, paleness, depressed state.
Cause: A worm that moves through the gastrointestinal tract of the peafowl. Spread through the environment and from bird to bird.
Treatment: Treatment is done with wormers.
Vaccination: No, de worming twice a year with Thiabendazole, Tramisol, Fenbandazole, or Ivermactin is important.

Gape Worms
Symptoms: Respiratory problems, secondary infections, respiratory distress.
Cause: A worm that moves into the trachea of the peafowl. Spread through improper hygiene in the pens and has been linked to earthworms as well.
Treatment: Treatment is done with Tramisol and/or Thiabendazole
Vaccination: No, de-worming twice a year can help prevent.

Mites

Symptoms: Itching, restlessness, over preening

Cause: Mites are a small external parasite that eat skin, scales and feather debris. Spread from bird to bird and more commonly seen in peafowl that roam.

Treatment: Treatment with a pesticide 3 or 4 times every 10 days. Make sure that treatment is bird safe.

Coccidiosis

Coccidiosis is a devastating disease caused by single-cell parasites called coccidia. Outbreaks occur in commercial and domestic flocks the world over. The organisms live inside the gut walls of infested peacocks, other poultry, wild birds and even cats and dogs. Coccidiosis can be fatal if left untreated.

Coccidiosis prevention measures

• Avoid overcrowding in peacock enclosures.

• Change water in drinkers at least once a day.

• Add apple cider vinegar to the drinking water.

• Give your birds garlic, fresh green leaves, comfrey, and cod liver oil.

• Do everything you can to keep the floor of the peacock coop clean and dry.

Coccidia is host-specific, which means those that infected turkeys, for example, can't be transferred to peacocks or vice versa. Coccidia strains affect mostly bird species, but some are capable of using other animals as hosts.

The symptoms of coccidiosis in peacocks

Coccidiosis infests peacocks of any age. In very young chicks, however, there are no symptoms at all because the parasites are not yet present in sufficient numbers to manifest visible problems. Identification of coccidiosis can be challenging because some of the symptoms can be caused by various mineral and vitamin deficiencies and can be present with a variety of diseases and disorders.

The most common symptom is diarrhea, which may or may not contain blood. The worse the infection gets, the more severe diarrhea becomes; it is accompanied by white sticky smears around the vent area, on the skin and tangled up in the feathers. Infested birds can appear depressed, unresponsive and lethargic. They will also have untidy-looking feathers and show no interest in food or mating. Hens eventually stop producing eggs altogether. The peacock's eyes may be closed, and feathers can be lost. Young birds and chicks may stop growing or develop much more slowly than expected.

Coccidiosis can be fatal if left untreated. Unfortunately, it is often noticed when birds do begin to die as a result of infestation. Peacocks can develop resistance to the organism when it is present in their environment in deficient concentrations. When birds become old or sick because of unrelated diseases, coccidia can take advantage of an already stressed immune system and begin to multiply in the host's gut.

How coccidiosis spreads
The primary means of coccidia transmission is by birds eating the droppings of other birds that are already infested. The droppings contain oocysts (a stage in the development of coccidia), which must mature before they can be transmitted to other birds. This can happen in 24 hours, but the oocysts can stay alive inside a peacock coop, outside of a host, for well over 12 months.

Droppings
Accidental or deliberate consumption of droppings is a common occurrence and cannot be stopped. The droppings may be from other peacocks in the enclosure. They could also be from wild birds, which cannot be entirely excluded as potential sources of infestation unless the peacocks are kept in a covered run that wild birds cannot get into.

Treatment
If a coccidiosis outbreak is suspected, you should consult a vet immediately. Droppings can quickly be analyzed in a laboratory to

determine the presence of coccidia, and treatment can start as soon as a positive result is confirmed. In situations where the peacock-keeper is confident (often from experience) that coccidia is present, a vet needn't be called in, or tests carried out because the necessary treatments are available without a prescription.

Antibiotics are useless against this parasite. Treatment involves a coccidiostat medicine, which is added to the birds' drinking water for a set period. During this period any eggs produced cannot be consumed and must be safely disposed of. Administering the medicine is easy. However, during an outbreak, you also have to kill the oocysts that are inside the coop and on the ground inside the peacock run. The housing will need to be thoroughly and painstakingly scrubbed with a cleaning product that contains a coccidiostat chemical agent.

You should be able to use the same product in a watering can and apply it directly to the ground. Just make sure that you do this immediately after the peacocks have gone to bed and didn't wash it away. It follows that you should check the weather forecast beforehand. If it is going to rain or snow not long after the treatment has been applied, do it anyway but be prepared to do it again and again until dry weather allows the chemicals to do their work without interruption.

Any eggs laid by treated hens should not be consumed during treatment and for 28 days afterward. This is to allow time for the medication to leave the birds' systems altogether and so not find its way into eggs intended for humans. The same rule applies to birds that are to be slaughtered for table – not that a keeper of pet peacocks is going to do that, but it needs to be stated.

Do not give your peacocks any supplementary vitamins or minerals during treatment, as these could interact with the coccidiostat medicine and make it less efficient.

Scaly Leg

Breeds with feathered legs, such as Silkies or Pekins, are said to be more susceptible to scaly leg mite infestations. However, last time I checked, scaly leg mites express no preference and will strike any peacock. They are equal-opportunity pests.

Scaly leg is as horrible as it sounds: a parasite causes the scales on a peacock's legs to peel back, bleed and become very sore. Thankfully, this is easy enough to treat.

This relatively common affliction is caused by a parasite called Knemidocoptes mutants. The mites are invisible to the human eye. When it comes to choosing where to eat, these parasites usually prefer the legs of peacocks (hence the name), but they can also be found dining out on combs and wattles. Unlike red mite, scaly leg mite doesn't wander away from the table. It spends its entire life munching on the peacock and spreads by direct contact between birds in a flock.

Symptoms
Scaly leg mite itself is invisible to the naked eye, but the effects of an infestation are easy to see. The scales on a peacock's leg will no longer be smooth. They will stick out, and they can sometimes appear to be crusty and white.

If left untreated, scaly leg mites cause immense discomfort and irritation, and they can ultimately result in infested birds becoming permanently lame.

Treatment
Back in my early days as a peacock-keeper, a keeper with a lifetime of experience told me that one sure-fire way of killing scaly leg mite was to use white spirit. "You apply it to the peacocks' feet," he said. "And don't wash it off." Don't ever use white spirit. It will burn your sick peacock and significantly increase its suffering, albeit temporarily. I still don't know if it's even effective, and I don't intend to try to find out by testing it on any of my hens!

Modern treatments don't involve inflicting additional pain to your infested birds. The easiest thing to try is petroleum jelly. Smear it onto the affected bird's legs and reapply it every few days for three weeks. It is to ensure you break the life cycle of the site; any of the blighters that hatch out after the initial application will be quickly suffocated.

However, for ease of use and effectiveness, I recommend using Ivermectin. It's a spot-on treatment that is applied in the same way as those used to prevent fleas in dogs and cats. You simply part a peacock's feathers, ideally at the base of the neck, and apply a few drops of the stuff directly onto the skin. You might need to repeat the treatment.

In some countries, this broad-spectrum anti-parasitic medicine is not available without a prescription, and it is not licensed for use in poultry (although it is available to buy online). As with any medication you are not familiar with, you should consult your vet before using it. If your vet is not in favor of using Ivermectin, an alternative will be recommended.

Red Mite at Night

Red mites will feed on peacocks of any age. Even youngsters bursting with curiosity and life can quickly go downhill and die if an infestation goes untreated. Unfortunately, peacocks face a genuine and constant threat from these nighttime bloodsuckers in the spring and summer months. Such an invasion is every peacock keeper's worst nightmare. These tiny monsters can pour out of every nook and cranny inside a coop, sometimes numbering in their millions. Getting rid of them can be a real challenge.

Because their names are similar, the red spider mite and the red mite are often confused. They are nothing like each other, though. While the red spider mite feeds on plant sap and is often found in greenhouses, the red poultry mite, Dermanyssus gallinae, gorges itself on the blood of your peacocks.

The life cycle of an individual red mite is just one week, but it can lay many hundreds of eggs in that short period. An infestation often goes unnoticed at first because red mite emerges only under cover of darkness to feed, vanishing into every nook and cranny they can find inside the coop during daylight hours.

These mites aren't red unless they've recently fed. The red color is the blood of your peacocks. They are an off-white or gray otherwise. They're smaller when they haven't had a feed, appearing like a bad case of dandruff at the ends of perches and in the nesting boxes.

Hard to see
Even the most fastidious keeper can fail to spot the tell tale signs of mite activity when cleaning the coop. A coop can appear bug-free one weekend; the next you can have hundreds of thousands (even millions) of these creatures pouring out when you open the coop up for cleaning.

Do you have an irrational fear of spiders? Trust me: these things will make your flesh crawl much worse than any eight-legged bathtub visitor. Red mite can't survive for very long on humans, but that doesn't mean they won't bite you. They will. Some people suffer allergic reactions to them, so it's a perfect idea to keep some antihistamine medications around.

Even as I type these words, I can feel myself starting to itch all over. I have had personal experience of dealing with these horrors, and I know just how persistent they can be. You think you've finally killed them all, but you check inside the coop a few days later, and it's like they never went away. Your luck can change too. I had no encounters with red mite during my first three years of keeping peacocks, and then – wham! – I had an infestation of Biblical proportions to contend with.

At least the nasty blighters are inactive during the cold winter months. They tend to be around from May through to October. Although it's difficult to eradicate them, it isn't impossible. The only way to defeat red mite is to wage a brutal war against them. There can be only one victor – and that's you, the peacock-keeper.

Symptoms
A red mite is only 0.7mm in length. You've as much chance of spotting them in small numbers as you have of hearing Big Ben chime the hour in London from across the Atlantic. What you need to look for is evidence of red mite activity, not the mites themselves. However, if you've already got a well-established colony, there's no mistaking the red and gray seething masses for anything else.

Red mites leave behind a gray, ashy deposit that accumulates around the ends of perches. If you lift the poles, you're certain to see groups of insects milling around. It is because the pole ends allow easy access to the roosting peacocks at night.

Another way to identify a red mite problem is to observe the behavior of your peacocks. For reasons unknown, some will be getting bitten more than others. Those suffering the most will sometimes refuse to go to bed at night and will linger in the coop doorway. They can develop pale combs and anemia. Many hens stop laying. You might find red smears of blood on any eggs that do get laid; these are squashed mites. If the infestation is left to run riot, fatalities are inevitable; these are caused by blood loss and secondary infections.

When cleaning a mite-infested coop, you should wear protective clothing that can be easily removed and bundled immediately into a washing machine when you're done. The last thing anyone wants is for these nasty things to get into your house.

Thick rubber or plastic garden gloves are essential.

When entering the coop, be mindful that red mites are probably everywhere, including above your head. You'll find that even if not a single bug finds its way onto you, you'll still want to run straight for the shower when you've finished cleaning. It's wise to do so, not only for peace of mind but also to ensure you aren't carrying any of the mites on you.

Get the mix right
Specialized cleaning products marketed as red mite killers are available from your local feed supplier. These are usually in concentrated form, and you mix them with water. Always ensure you add the correct amount of cleaner to the water, as detailed on the packaging.

Remove all the old soiled bedding from the coop and dispose of it. When dealing with an infestation, it's unwise to put the litter on your compost heap. You should burn it or bag it up and take it away. Remove the perches and clean them somewhere else (well away from your peacocks). Apply the mite-killing mix to the poles and everywhere inside the coop. Leave the solution to do its work for however long the manufacturer stipulates.

When the required time has elapsed, get a wire brush and scrub the perches and inside the coop as you've never scrubbed anything before. Pay particular attention to the nesting boxes, hard-to-reach places, the ends of the perches and the slots the poles fit into. If you miss any part, you can be darn sure that will be where red mite survivors are hiding.

Be thorough. If you're not, you won't win the war.

Rinse away
When you're done scrubbing, it's time to clean the coop. Thank goodness red mites aren't a winter problem because it takes an hour or two for a coop to dry out, even at the height of summer.

Somewhere to lay: If your hens are getting antsy because they want to lay eggs while all this cleaning work is going on, they'll let you know. You could provide them with a clean enclosed cat-litter tray filled with their usual nesting box material. Just put it on the ground, and they'll almost certainly know what you've provided it for. Don't forget to take it away when the coop is once again open for business.

Diatomaceous earth is an incredibly useful material for keeping coops dry and killing insects, including parasites such as red mite. Before the peacocks are allowed back inside the coop, you should dust them directly with diatomaceous earth and liberally shake it into every nook and cranny inside the coop, again paying particular attention to nesting boxes, the ends of the perches and the supporting slots. You should grind the powder in wherever you can. The conventional bedding material can go in afterward.

Okay, you can breathe easy now. You're finished. Well, not quite. You will need to do this every three days, for three weeks. All being well, you'll break the life cycle of the red mites in this time, killing newly hatched beasties before they get a chance to repopulate.

Are you scratching yourself now? I wouldn't be surprised.

Mites and Lice

Recognizing Mites: some mites are visible, and the symptoms are easy to spot: Restlessness or listlessness, preening, sometimes feathers will be missing, and bald spots occur. Birds may avoid going into their nesting house. You can check the room for the little red buggers.

Lice can be seen when feathers are pulled apart – eggs are usually laid near the vent area of the birds and are attached to the feather shaft.

Mites can be treated with Scalex Mite spray, Avian Insect Liquidator or Scatt (moxidectin). DE can be used to dust the birds for both mites and lice. Keeping a dust bath area open for your birds is important to prevent infestations. Cleaning roosts and nesting boxes and treating the bedding is important. Spray a mite/lice killer into all the cracks of the nesting area and housing.

Make sure to wash your clothes immediately (changing outdoors if possible) as the mites can spread to humans.

Safety concerns

While for most people it is enough to keep a clean coop and wash their hands after handling peacocks some people have a suppressed immune system, or conditions such as asthma, which means extra precautions are needed.

While it is not common for people to contract illness from live peacocks, the possibility remains. Diseases such as salmonella, bird flu, and histoplasmosis have been associated with being in contact with peacocks. If you or someone in your household is prone to disease, the following points will help reduce the risks.

Wash Your Eggs

Rinse any eggs you gather gently using warm soapy water. Don't immerse them in hot water.

Rinse them off with clean water before storing. It is important to note that when you wash your eggs this will also remove the natural coating on them, which will reduce their shelf life so enjoy them as soon as possible.

Wash Your Hands
Whenever you handle anything to do with peacocks, make sure you wash your hands afterward.

Keep Your Flock Away From Other People's Birds

If your peacocks remain healthy, there is less chance of them spreading the disease to you.

To reduce the possibility of diseases spreading between your birds or other people's birds, don't let your peacocks mix with other people's birds and don't share drinkers, feeders or any other equipment which has been used by someone else to tend to their flock.

Wear A Dust Mask
It is especially important for people with lung or respiratory issues. Peacocks can create a lot of dust, which is also a good reason to ensure that your coop is properly ventilated. Wear a dust mask whenever you are in your coop for more than a few seconds. Dust masks can be very affordable and are available at most supermarkets and hardware stores.

Change Your Clothes after Working in your Coop
Because there is usually dust and dirt on your clothes after you have finished working on your coop, it is a good idea to have a clean set of clothes ready, so when you're done, you can change your clothes. Make sure you wash your soiled clothes as soon as possible.

Keep a spare pair of shoes for working in your peacock coop.

Supervise Children Around Your Peacocks
Never allow young unsupervised children around your peacocks. For young children, there are physical dangers around peacocks, such as an aggressive rooster. Also, young children tend to put their hands in their

mouths, so make sure they wash their hands after handling peacocks to prevent them from contracting any peacock-related illnesses.

Monitor Your Flock

When caring for any animals, a watchful eye is critical. Pay close attention to how your birds behave and look. If something appears to be unusual, take immediate action. If you have a sick hen, isolate her from the rest of the flock until the problem has been remedied.

Chapter 7. Feeding Your Peacock

Feeding your peafowl is not actually that difficult, since they thrive on common bird mixes that you would feed peahens or even wild birds. That being said, there are a few things that you should consider and in this chapter I will go over everything you need to know to properly feed your peafowl and peacocks.

The Basic Peacock Diet

Generally, if you are looking for food, you should choose a blend that is better formulated for other birds, or more specifically for quail. Although they are not a complete match, quail are very close to peafowl and their feed is much better for peafowl than any other type of feed.

Before I get into depth about what you need to feed your peafowl, I should point out that there are many different opinions on what is best for your peafowl. The recommendations in this book are considered to be the best diet; however, peafowl can thrive on a variety of mixtures so I always recommend discussing diet with your peafowl breeder before you bring your bird home.

When it comes to looking at peafowl, owners should realize that peafowl are omnivores. This means that they eat seeds, vegetation and meat, or rather insects and do not solely eat manufactured foods. I will go over supplements later on in this chapter but when you are planning your diet, try to take their omnivorous diet into consideration.

That being said, you can also choose peahen food. There are a few peafowl feeds available but they are fairly difficult to come by depending on where you live.

Peacocks need a higher protein level than peahens. Free range birds will naturally get enough protein if you have a large bug population. We use peafowl feed, as it is higher in protein than peahen feed. Our peacocks love table scraps and other non-commercial food. When feeding the birds leftovers – make sure to watch that you do not use overly salty foods like potato chips, or sugary cereals.

Here are some details of what you can do for your peafowl's diet:
Rice, Bread, strawberry tops, watermelon without the rind, eggshells that have been dried and crumbled, celery tops, arugula and black sunflower seeds are favorites for our birds. Remember that rice can be empty calories if it is only white rice.

- Adding oyster shells or dried and crumbled egg shells can provide some extra minerals and calcium.

- Make a mash of fermented rice or oatmeal. The fermentation and partial sprouting is great for humans and birds.

- Corn heats up the metabolism of the bird so avoid it during hot summers. On hot days sometimes some frozen fruit cubes (ice cube trays) will be very welcomed by your peacock.

- Feeding scrap draws flies; have good fly prevention in place. Try covering your scraps with a light dusting of food grade Diatomaceous Earth. Fruits and veggies seem to make them happy. I generally remove pits and the rinds to keep cleanup easy.

- Free offering of garlic cloves and a free offering of cayenne pepper (great benefits for preventing worms) will allow your birds to self-medicate.

- Treats like cat or dog food pellets, or cooked egg yolks are higher in protein.

Water Details

Feeders and professional water containers can be hung or alternatively a five gallon bucket of water can be used. The bucket can be attached to the side of the cage with zip ties – just drill a couple of small holes in the top of the bucket above your fill line. Clean weekly with a mild bleach solution or just use plain hot water and a toilet brush that bought and used strictly for the birds' container clean up.

Food and water for your group of exotic birds is fairly easy. Once you set up your food and water stations in the coop or in a place that the free range birds can access easily – you can simply clean out the containers once a week and add nutrients as needed.

In the water you can add electrolytes or vitamins on a schedule you or your vet determine is best. Some owners add vinegar to the water swearing that it prevents diseases while others say there is no proven benefit to adding it. I like to add 5 tablespoons of Apple Cider Vinegar (Braggs is in the health food sections at some local grocery stores) to our five gallon pail of water at least once a month. Some people put in a splash of vinegar every day. Some owners alternate with Lactic Acid Bacteria (LAB).

Algae growth can be reduced by adding little burlap bags filled with barley straw to your water containers. Those bags work decently to reduce the algae and can be found at feed stores or online at livestock supply websites like Tractor Supply Company. You can also make them yourself. Some people prefer to use Diatomaceous Earth or DE (food grade only) in the water to reduce algae and prevent worms in the peafowl.

Other foods

Quail Feed
The majority of your feed will be the quail feed and usually consists of a blend of seeds and grains that benefit the bird. It is important that you choose a quail feed that has kelp meal in it. Make sure that the kelp meal is raw and that it provides a high source of keratin. If the food does not, either order kelp meal and add about one part to two parts of feed to your food or find a different feed.

Bird Seeds
Seeds are very important for your peafowl's diet and a blend of natural seeds and grains that are made for wild birds is a good choice. Choose one that is just a blend with a range of grains and seeds and does not have any fillers or preservatives. Organic and all natural products are the best for your birds.

When you combine these two feeds, use two parts quail feed and one part bird seed. Give the feed to your birds on a daily basis.

The amount differs depending on several factors including:

- How many birds you have.
- If they are free ranging or if they are kept in a pen.
- Their age.
- The season.

Although the feed makes up a large part of their diet, you should never keep your peafowl on the feed alone. Peafowl have a large appetite and if they are free ranging birds you will find that they will usually cover many of the needs of their diet. However, if they live in a pen, especially if it is an earth floor pen, you will need to provide them with much of their ranging needs.

Regardless, there are a number of different items that you should offer your peafowl on a regular basis.

Meat

As I have mentioned, peafowl are omnivores so they do require some meat based protein in their diets. In fact, about 20% of the peafowl's diet should be protein. The best choice for this is a wet dog food.

Twice a week, break up two or three large cans of wet dog food. Simply toss it into the pen or around the area where your peafowl usually feed. The birds will scratch around for the food and will receive enough protein for the week.

Another source of meat can be worms or grubs. If you do purchase these, make sure that the insects are not invasive species as insects can get out of the pens. Simply toss the insects into the pen.

Fruit

Cut open the fruit so the peafowl can get at the soft fruit and seeds inside. You can also cut it into very small bits and toss it into the pen so the peafowl can scratch for it. If you do this, make sure that you consider the size of their beaks so the food is not too difficult for them to swallow. Although fruit is not usually added to the regular feed, it should be offered to your peafowl on a regular basis. This will help the birds get a well-blended diet and will ensure that they get enough vitamins and minerals.

One thing that you should note is that peafowl usually only dig through fruit for the seeds and don't usually eat it but some types of fruit they will eat.

Some types of fruit that peafowl like are:
• Melons: Any type of melon is a good choice for peafowl. Make sure you cut this open and just set it in the pen. The peafowl will do the rest.

• Berries: Ranging peafowl will often find berries to eat on their own but blueberries, raspberries and strawberries can be a nice treat for the birds.

• Grapes: Many peafowl will eat the whole fruit.

• Citrus Fruit: Again, cut citrus fruit open and simply leave them out for the birds to eat.

• Pumpkin: Pumpkin has often been identified as a natural wormer and is an excellent choice during the winter.

Greens and Vegetables
If you can't keep grass growing in the pens, which can be very difficult, make sure that you offer your peafowl greens and some types of vegetables. Again, most of these do not need to be broken down but simply cut open in the case of hard shelled vegetables. Make sure you offer vegetables two or three times a week.

If you have the ability to do this, try to keep grass growing in your pens since peafowl will eat snippets of the grass and you won't need to add a lot of different vegetables and greens to their diet.

• Plants: You can offer plant snippings. I have provided you with a list of plants and flowers that peafowl find appetizing in the section on range feeding.

• Lettuce: Lettuce and other green leafy vegetables are good for peafowl.

• Squash: Like pumpkins, squash is an excellent winter treat and it can be used as a natural wormer.

Grains

In fact, the more variety you have in your peafowl's diet, the better your peafowl's health will be. This will translate into happier birds that have better colouring and will also help your bird's fertility. While your peafowl will receive a fair amount of their grain intake in their feed, you can also offer them breads, rice and other grain products throughout the year. This provides them with variety and the birds enjoy getting treats.

In addition to these foods, you can also offer things like cheese to your peafowl and there really aren't too many restrictions.

When you feed your birds, remember that peafowl usually forage for food in the early morning and late afternoon, usually right before sunset. Plan to feed your birds at this time.

Range Feeding

When a peacock or peafowl is free ranging, they have a wide variety of food available to them. Although their primary diet is seeds and the quail feed that you provide them, they will also eat insects, small animals and even snakes. In fact, peafowl will eat just about anything and they can even eat poisonous snakes.

If we are looking at range feeding peafowl, you aren't going to make a lot of changes to the overall diet. Generally, the range feeding birds will have access to all the extra foods; however, you want to make sure that you offer the same opportunities for fruit, meat and vegetables.

The main difference is that you will need to find an ideal spot to feed your range feeding birds as opposed to the ones kept in a pen.

Peacocks will also eat plants that you have in and around your property. Be sure to fence off or screen your garden, as peafowl will find their way into it. While they may focus on the bugs, some of your flowers and plants may seem too tempting to leave alone so be prepared for them to be eaten.

Another point that you should consider is a free ranging bird will forage away from your property so make sure that your surrounding neighbours are okay with having a peacock eating their plants.

One thing that you should be aware of is that peafowl are often described as the goat of the bird world. They will eat just about anything so make sure that your yard is free of manmade hazards. Things like Styrofoam pellets, plastic caps and small pieces of fabric can all be ingested by the birds and will make them sick or result in death.

For the rest, let your birds take care of their feeding and you will find that by providing enough variety to your regular feed, on top of what they are foraging, your birds will be healthy and happy with a splendid display of colour.

Plants Peafowl Eat
Below is a list of plants that peafowl enjoy eating. Make sure that you offer a few of these plants as having more foraging in your own yard and garden will keep the peafowl on your property more.

Seedlings: First, any type of young plant or seedling is a popular treat for ranging peafowl. If you have a few plants that you want to keep safe, cover them until they are large enough so that the peafowl will ignore them.

Flowers: Flowers are not actually eaten but tend to be decimated for various reasons. The bird may be looking for insects or looking for seeds. Sometimes, peafowl will simply destroy a flower out of boredom.

While any type of flower can fall prey to a peafowl, some that they really enjoy are:
- Amaryllis
- Begonia
- Impatiens
- Pansy
- Petunia
- Primrose

Fruit and vegetables: While a garden can be a wonderful place for your peafowl to roam since there is an abundance of bugs, they will also devour some of your fruit and vegetables.

Some fruit vegetables that they eat are:

- Brussels Sprouts
- Cabbage
- Cauliflower
- Chives
- Lettuce
- Tomato
- Spinach
- Berry Plants: Any type of berry plant will catch your peafowl's interest but they are fond of Holly and also Blackberry and Blueberry.

Supplements

Before you decide whether to give your peafowl additional vitamins and minerals, make sure you speak with your veterinarian. Follow his recommendations. If you do not use vitamins and minerals, make sure the following foods are available to your peafowl on a regular basis to ensure they get everything they need.

When it comes to supplementing your peafowl's diet, there really isn't much that you need to add. Remember that a diet that is full of variety will have enough vitamins and minerals in the food to make sure that the birds stay healthy.

Kale: Raw kale is bursting with vitamins and is a good source of fibre for your birds. Try to offer a cup of minced kale every day.

Mushrooms: Again, these are full of minerals and vitamins and you should try to feed your peafowl mushrooms about one to three times per week.

Shrimp: Make sure the shrimp has its shell since it is the shell that you want your peafowl to eat. The amino acids in the shrimp will help with digestion. Offer your birds two or three shrimp per week.

Sweet Potato: Cook the sweet potato and offer it to the birds in its skin once a week. It is rich in vitamins and minerals.

Walnuts: Walnuts are an excellent source of vitamin E and should be fed twice a week. Only feed about two walnut pieces per bird.

Bamboo Shoots: Purchase canned bamboo as it is softer. These are full of minerals and vitamins. Feed one to three times per week.

Banana: The older the banana, the better, but bananas are a good source of potassium. Feed half a banana per bird, soaked, twice a week.

Celery: Feed celery to your peafowl about 5 times per week. Celery has been linked to a better digestive system in peafowl.

Chickpeas: Do not feed your peafowl manufactured chickpeas, instead, soak the chickpeas on your own and add them to the daily feed or use them as a treat. One cup of chickpeas offers your bird enough minerals to cover the daily suggested amount and have 10 different vitamins to increase their health.

Frogs Legs: Peafowl will often eat small lizards and amphibians when they are foraging and you can offer them frogs legs once a week for an alternative to their protein intake.

In addition to these supplements to your peafowl's diet, make sure you offer your peafowl fresh water every day and try to place the water on the ground. Hanging waterers are not appropriate for peafowl.

Lastly, make sure your peafowl has an opportunity to eat gravel from time to time to help with their digestion.

Feeding Peachicks

For their diet, I do recommend that you start the peachicks on a quail starter diet or a peafowl starter diet. You can then place them on a grower feed but generally, if you follow a diverse diet for your peafowl, you really don't need to make too many accommodations for the young.

In general, there isn't much that you need to do with your peachicks when it comes to feeding. Peahens are very good mothers and will often take over the care of the chicks at an early stage.

By three days old, the peachicks will begin to forage on their own and during this time, make sure you offer them a larger quantity of meat and protein based foods. After a few weeks they will begin to eat more greens and grains but during the initial growth their diet will consist of a high protein level. You should try to offer them a diet where 30% of their daily feed is protein based and then slowly reduce it down to the 20% by the time they are a few months old.

While it does seem like there is a lot to do with feeding your peafowl, really, it is not that difficult and you can simply place the food out for the birds. If you use more of the supplements for your birds, make sure that you also remove some of the empty calories. Things like bread and cheese aren't really needed and it is better to fill up your bird's diet with the healthier selections.

Chapter 8. Nesting And Breeding The Peacock

For those that are not free ranging, you will have to plan out your breeding to ensure that you get exactly what you want. In this chapter, I will go over everything you need to know about hatching and raising your own peachicks.

For many people, breeding peafowl becomes a hobby that they never intended to get into. The main reason for having a peafowl was simply to enjoy the birds and the eggs and breeding simply came as a result of owning both peacocks and peahens.

Left on their own, peafowl will multiply quite quickly if they are given the proper food and care during the months. In fact, many free ranging birds will produce their own peachicks without your aid and you can often be surprised by the sudden appearance of the young.

Breeding

With males, never try to breed them until they are 2 years of age and it is often better to wait until they are 3 years of age. Some peafowl, including the green peafowls, take longer to mature so don't worry if your peafowl are not producing until they are older.

The very first step to breeding peafowl is to select the proper birds for the laying season. Generally, most species of peafowl are mature by 2 years of age, but some have been known to produce eggs by a year. Although you can get eggs from some birds when they are 1 year old, I strongly recommend that you wait until the peahens are 2 or 3 years of age.

When you are choosing your breeding stock, there are a few things you should look for:

• Overall Health: The birds should appear healthy. Eyes should be clear, firm flesh and musculature, bright feathers, alert and curious. If they are not, you may have an illness in your birds that should be addressed first.

- Temperament: Although this isn't usually as important as health, you will want to have a peacock with good temperament. The more aggressive a peacock is, the better a breeder he is. You want a peacock with a good aggression level but not so aggressive that he makes it difficult for you to get in and manage your peafowl.

- With all of your breeding stock, take the time to have health tests done. If you have not read it, read the chapter on caring for your birds to determine what health problems are transferred to the chicks. It can be devastating to watch all of your peachicks succumb to an illness.

Once you have all the proper clearances and you have decided on the birds, you simply need to place them into pens together.

Mating starts in early spring and a male peacock can be placed with about 5 peahens and produce a good clutch of eggs.

All new breeders should note that usually the first year of laying is a small clutch; however, the second year is much larger.

Laying
What you do need to worry about is the eggs falling onto debris, including droppings. Under the roosting area, place straw or hay so the eggs have something soft to land on. In addition, keep the area very clean and remove any debris or faeces on a daily basis.

Laying usually begins sometime in April and the peahen will produce a number of eggs throughout the spring and summer months.
Generally, a hen will roost and then lay the eggs or she will lay the eggs onto the grounds. Do not be worried if she lays the eggs from a height of about 4 feet off the ground, as the eggs will usually survive a fall of that distance.

If you are allowing the peahen to sit on the eggs herself, you should expect 2 clutches of eggs at the most over the spring and summer
months. Generally, a peahen will lay 5 to 10 eggs in each clutch, although occasionally you will see larger clutches.

If you are incubating the eggs, then the peahen will usually produce eggs every other day for the entire breeding season, usually up to about 30 eggs, although some produce more. You may find that occasionally she will have a few days without production but generally she will start up again after a few days.

Incubation

Before breeding season, prepare your incubators. Clean them thoroughly so there is no chance of cross contamination from previous years. In addition, set the incubator in a room where you have a consistent temperature. Although the incubator has its own environment, placing it in a room that is too cold or too hot can affect the hatching.

Another important part of incubation is to have the proper humidity levels. Generally, humidity should be at about 80 to 88% and the humidity level should be adjusted to accommodate that. Purchase a hygrometer, which gauges the humidity, and take into account that the humidity in the room that may affect the incubator.

Once the incubator is ready and the peahens are laying their eggs, you can start collecting the eggs. Some points to remember when collecting are: Do not stack too many eggs together. The weight of the top eggs can crush the bottom eggs so only make the depth three or four eggs deep.

Mark each egg. When collecting from multiple pens, number the pens and then write the number on each of the eggs with pencil. Do not use markers as the ink can seep through the egg shell and kill the growing chick. Mark the egg in several locations so you don't have to worry about the number rubbing off.

Date the eggs. Remember to place a date on each egg as well or have a chart where you assign numbers to the date collected and pens. This will help keep things in order.

Now that the eggs are laid, it is time for incubation. As I have mentioned, if the peahen is sitting on the eggs herself, then you should only expect 1 to 2 clutches of eggs.

Incubation for peafowl is between 27 to 29 days and it can vary depending on the species, which is included in a chart at the end of this section. If you decide to incubate the eggs using an incubator, then you will need to plan for this. Make sure that you have a high quality incubator for your eggs as well as a hatcher.

Next, set up the incubator so that it has a temperature of about 99 to 100°F. If you can, purchase a model with an air circulation fan to ensure the temperature stays even. You should also check the temperature in several spots on your incubator to make sure there is an even distribution of heat.

One tip that works really well for incubation is to have the door of the incubator open slightly. This allows fresh air to pass through the incubator and it is very important for the development of the peachicks.

Search through the pen. Some peahens will cover up their eggs when they hatch them so make sure you thoroughly search through the pen.

Once you get the eggs, look through them and remove any that have been cracked when the peahen was laying them. For the rest, you can either wait to put them in the incubator or set them in.

If you choose to wait, keep the eggs at 55 to 60°F with no humidity. You can hold them for about 7 days after laying but never wait longer than that or you will not have a viable egg after that time.

For the ones that go into an incubator, place them on their sides in the incubator tray and point the tip downwards slightly.

As the eggs are incubating, it is very important to maintain the humidity and the temperature. In addition, the eggs should be turned every 2 to 2 hours by about 45° for proper development.

During incubation time, candle the eggs about once a week to check for fertility. Eggs that have no signs of fertility for 10 days should be removed as they will not develop into chicks.

To candle an egg:

1. Place a bare light bulb with a drop cord inside a cardboard box.
2. Cut a hole in the cardboard box that is about ½ an inch in diameter.
3. Seal the rest of the box.
4. Turn off the light in the room if possible.

Take an egg and holding it on the top and bottom, place it against the hole so the light shines through the egg. You should be able to see the yolk and the chick depending on the stage of development.

If an egg is infertile, you will simply see a clear egg and a shadow where the yolk is. This is an egg that should be removed from the incubator, although you should wait at least 10 days before you remove it. A fertilized egg should have a spider like shape in the candled egg. This is the embryo and the blood vessels moving out from it.

An egg where the embryo has died is called a dead germ egg and when this occurs, you will see the spider like embryo but you will also see a ring of blood around the embryo. This is caused by the blood moving away from the embryo after death. Any dead germ eggs should be removed.
Eggs that are fertile should go back to incubation and as the peachick develops you may start seeing the chick form and possibly move inside the egg.

Hatching
Generally, the eggs are moved to a hatcher when they are 25 to 26 days in incubation. Temperature levels in the hatcher should be kept at the same 99 to 100°F level but the humidity should be raised slightly, usually keeping it closer to 88%.

Hatching usually begins between 27 to 29 days after the eggs have been set on but before that occurs there is a very important step that breeders should take and that is not turning the eggs.

The eggs should not be turned during this time, as turning will prevent the chick from orienting itself for hatching.

After two or three days in the hatcher, the chicks will begin to hatch. It is important to leave the chick in the hatcher for an additional day after hatching to give it time to stand up on its own and begin moving around.

Young Peachicks

After they have been hatched, remember to let the peachick stay in the hatcher for an extra day. Once that time has passed, move the peachick to a brooder that has a similar temperature and humidity level as the hatcher. One thing that I strongly recommend is to have several brooders. This way you can move the peachicks to a different room as they age so they stay with other peachicks their size. This prevents younger peachicks from not being injured and you can slowly decrease the temperature from room to room.

Caring for your young peachicks can be fairly simple and it really depends on whether or not you are raising the chicks on your own.

If your peafowl set the eggs herself, then simply leave the peachicks with her. She will see that they are getting fed and will keep them safe.

Although some breeders disagree, in most cases, peahens are amazing mothers. The only real concern that you should take is keeping the peachicks safe from predators since peahens nest on the ground. The best way to do this is to keep the peahens penned during nesting.

If the peachicks are incubated in an incubator, then you will need to do a bit more work with them.

Keep the peachicks inside the brooders for roughly 10 weeks, although I recommend trying to keep them in the brooders for about 12 weeks. During that time, clean the brooders on a daily basis to prevent diseases in your peachicks. In addition, make sure there is a constant supply of fresh, clean water for the peachicks to drink.

Start the peachicks on a starter feed and I recommend you read the chapter on peafowl diet to learn how to feed a peachick. However, start feeds should be stopped once the peachick is 6 months of age.

Once they are twelve weeks of age, you can begin moving them into juvenile pens and then finally allow them access to an outdoor pen. Do not allow a peachick to roam before it is a year old and has been properly conditioned.

Chapter 9. Reproduction – Incubation and Brooding The Peacock

Deciding whether to incubate or let your Peahen set on her eggs is a personal choice. We like the fun of interacting with the peachicks from day one. But we imagine it might be easier to allow the peahen to raise offspring, than intervening and raising the chicks yourself. The risk with a broody peahen is that predators may be attracted to the small chicks. Incubation can be rewarding. Here are the basics: incubate for 28 -29 days with 99-100 degree heat and about 85-88% humidity. If you do not have an incubator that turns the eggs, you must hand turn those eggs 2x a day. Marking one side (in pencil) with and "x" and the other with an "o" allowed us to easily track if the eggs were turned each day.

Set up an area of at least 20 square feet so that your peahen can lay her eggs and go broody in private. Use plenty of straw. A roost placed high up in the cage will allow your bird an escape if a predator does invade her turf. Surround your pen with non-toxic bushes that hide and shade your coop: Grapes, Bamboo, Maple Trees, Mock Orange, Baby's Breath, or Black-eyed Susan vines may camouflage the area enough to prevent close inspection by predators.

A day or two after hatching, we moved the chicks in homemade brooder, a large Rubbermaid container will house 2-4 baby chicks. Use newspaper or clean shavings and install a brooder light and thermometer to keep the temperature at about 95 -100 the first week. Reduce the temperature by 5 degrees per week. An alternative to the old fashioned brooder lamp is the EcoGlow 20 found on Amazon. I really would like to try this out. One of the breeders I know used it for peahens, but I am not sure how well it will translate to raising our peachicks.

Feeding the baby peachicks was a breeze. We used a blender to grind peafowl pellets and gave a sprinkle of cooked egg yolks for the first few days. We bought small shallow dishes from Goodwill and used the containers and lids for the water and food. You may have to teach them how to eat and drink their food at first, using your finger as an example.

And last, a small window screen may cover your container perfectly – allowing for good airflow and protection from the chicks flying up and out.

How to tell if a peacock is broody

• The hen becomes less sociable and more aggressive.

• She stays in the nesting box for extended periods of time, refusing to leave and growling (yes, growling!) at humans and other peacocks that come near.

• Brood patches can develop: parts of the breast and abdomen areas become featherless.

• The hen may eat and drink less.

• A bird is likely to be broody in spring and summer, but not in autumn and winter.

• The hen has stopped laying eggs but steals eggs from other birds and guards them jealously.

• A peacock will know what's going on even if you don't, and he won't try it on with the peacock for fear of his life! So be aware of the peacock's behavior if you have one.

• What breed is the hen? Read up on whether it's known to be inclined to go broody at the drop of a feather or not at all.

Why peacocks go broody

Sometimes a bird wants to sit/set on eggs and raise chicks, but the bird-keeper may not wish for that to happen and will seek to discourage brooding. This hormonally governed change in a hen happens only in the spring and summer months. It's a natural instinct and stronger in some birds than in others, just as the desire to have children differs between humans.

Adult hens start to go broody in the early spring, as the daylight hours grow longer. There is no hard and fast rule set by Mother Nature as to when this will happen, though.

The majority of birds stop eating or eat very little when they are broody. They only occasionally drink water and rarely leave the nest. When they do leave the nest, they produce the most horrible poops ever. Nothing smells quite so awful as a broody hen's poops. They are usually significantly larger decks than normal as well. It is all because of the hormonal storm raging inside the broody hen's body.

Broodiness lasts for three weeks (21 days) if a bird is allowed to sit on eggs. The broody state may go on for longer in persistent birds that either has not been allowed to sit or have been sitting on unfertilised eggs.

When broodiness is undesirable

If you want chicks at the same time as a hen becomes broody, this is all well and good, but there are many reasons why a hen sitting on eggs and rearing young may be undesirable. One reason is the unsuitability of a hen for motherhood if she belongs to a non-sitting breed, which means she might not be inclined to finish what she started, abandoning the nest and leaving the eggs to go cold and the chicks inside to die. Also, if the hen is very young and this is her first attempt at hatching eggs, she may get bored after a few days or, heartbreakingly, just a day or two before the eggs are due to hatch. She may just not yet fully know exactly what it is she's supposed to do.

If a hen does lose interest, there's no chance of you reigniting the bird's former enthusiasm. When it's gone, it's gone. It's a good idea to have an incubator running on standby, just in case disaster strikes.

You may have limited space in a backyard or garden, with no capacity to support a higher number of birds, even for a limited time; it takes several months for a chick to reach full saleable maturity. There's also the entirely understandable desire on the part of many keepers to avoid the possibility of needing to cull unwanted peacocks if homes can't be found for them.

Many keepers are highly selective about which hens in their flocks they allow to breed and raise young. They run focused breeding programs, in which the parents are carefully selected for a variety of attractive characteristics, such as physical attributes, temperament, and number of eggs laid annually. They have no interest in just allowing nature to take its course and produce undetermined hybrids (what dog owners call mongrels).

Can broodiness be prevented?
No, but you can try to stop it once it is under way. You do this because the broody state is very taxing; a hen's energy reserves can be depleted by sitting on a nest for a long time.

Some of the methods said to bring a peacock out of the broody state are very cruel and amount to torture. They cannot be recommended by any keeper of a clear conscience. These unacceptably harsh strategies invariably involve making a hen extremely distressed by keeping her rigidly confined and denying her access to food and water for days on end. Not only do the horrible methods not work most of the time, but they also risk causing physical and psychological harm to the hen. Stress alone can kill a bird.

What is to be recommended is removing the broody hen from the flock and keeping her in a separate area. This can be a large animal cage raised up on bricks, which ensures the hen cannot get sufficiently comfortable to nest, or a small coop, such as one of the types referred to as an 'ark.' This far more gentle hands-off approach allows the hen to steadily calm down from the agitated state that is typical of the open condition. The hen must continue to have access to water and food at all times during daylight hours. Any eggs she lays must be immediately removed, although she isn't at all likely to lay an egg when broody. If a hen is not unusually persistent, this is all that needs to be done for a day or two. With more determined broody hens, it may be necessary to continue with the separation for a while longer.

Why separate at all? Well, a broody hen will sit on any eggs, not just her own and, moreover, broodiness is catching. If a hen goes broody and isn't separated from her flock for a while, the chances are high that other birds will go the same way.

Some keepers recommend that you can try wetting the hen's belly and breast feathers with cold water (don't douse the poor girl in entirety) because a broody hen uses her body heat in those areas to warm her eggs. The cooling effect of the water, so the theory goes, will eventually put the bird off her grand idea of starting a family. Don't do this at all if the weather is anything less than hot and sunny, though, because you don't want the hen to catch a cold – or worse. I know of keepers who are totally against this, but my own opinion is that it isn't at all cruel to get a bit of water on a hen on a hot day. It's far crueler to leave a bird in that churning, anxious state of broodiness for weeks on end, without ever trying to get her mind away from the hormonal compulsion to become a parent.

There is no guaranteed quick and easy method to get a hen to stop being broody. What is certain is that she will, with patience and determination on the part of her keeper, lose interest and show signs of returning to her normal temperament and behaviors before too long; at that point, the hen can be safely returned to the flock. Don't be surprised if she goes broody again within just a few days or a week, though. Persistently broody hens can be very stressful for a keeper to deal with. Of course, you may want to let your broody hen sit on fertile eggs and raise some chicks, in which case you should read the next chapter straight away.

Protection from Predators

Make sure the whole coop and especially the peahen's area is safe from predators – which can include your cat or dog.

Here are some steps to protect against any predator, whether man or beast:
1. A radio turned on to your local talk radio station might ward off some predators that are afraid of the human voice.

2. Motion detector lights or a timer light that comes on automatically at dusk might help prevent animals from coming too close to your pen.

3. Planting shrubs around the cage or at least the nesting area of the pen will mask hens that are broody. Pay attention if you hear excess noise from the peafowl – as they do alert to danger.

4. You can keep some snakes away with reinforcing the outside bottom edge of the cage (sealing all gaps) and installing snake proof fencing. Tight, smooth mesh is best.

Make sure all the gaps are filled in on the cage itself. Check that all the peahen wire is free from damage. A weekly inspection to make sure there are no holes cracks, or weak areas developing will save you hours of time later on. Give plenty of high perches so that the bird can escape predators. Your peacock will have easy escape if the door is left open or does not latch properly. Do not leave the door open for even a few seconds while you enter the cage to retrieve bowls.

1. An outer fence can help prevent problems and a guard dog can be used to protect your peafowl.

2. Additionally you can set up a security camera system to monitor activity from within your home.

Chapter 10. Socializing Your Peacock

I have always felt that socializing your peafowl is just as important as socializing your dog. Peafowl that understand that you are not a threat are more likely to stay within sight of you and you will be able to enjoy them much more than if they stay hidden.

One area that is often up for debate is whether or not you really need to socialize your peacocks or peafowls. As I have mentioned several times throughout this book, peafowl are usually very standoffish birds and they don't really bond with their owners.

Creating a Friendlier Peacock

To promote this type of socialization, it is better to start with the bird as a chick:

• Hold it often. Make sure that you hold the chick on a daily basis, several times per day.

• Place it where there is human contact. Although you may not want it in the house, have the peachick as close to humans as possible so it rests and spends its day next to people.

• Hand feed the chick. Always feed the chick by hand. Like most animals, the more it sees you as a positive thing, such as a place to get food, the more likely it will come to you when it is older.

• Avoid corrections. Unlike a dog, a peachick is not going to learn commands and training. Remember that these are semi-wild animals and they will behave as such. Correcting the bird for doing something you view as wrong will only make the bird wary of you and the bird will avoid coming close.

One thing that should be mentioned is that this type of socialization can be both a positive and negative thing. On one hand, you may get a very tame peafowl that will even come up and perch on you. On the other hand, there have been cases of peafowl becoming aggressive to humans after socialization. The main reason why this occurs is because the bird starts to view you as one of its own species. Once it does this, it will start to view you as competition to its territory.

Peahens are usually much better to socialize than peacocks, as they tend to be less aggressive.

If you are purchasing an older bird, it is important to do your research. Make sure some socialization went into the raising of the bird.

Even if it did, you will need to take the time to really get to know the bird and get it to trust you. Always do this with food. Keep treats on hand and gradually throw the food closer to you so the bird needs to come closer to get the treat. Eventually, the bird will feel comfortable eating closer to you and will not view you as a threat to them.

The first thing that I should point out is that you should never expect to have a peacock or a peafowl that will come and sit on your lap and spend the day with you. There are the occasional stories about peafowl that are very friendly; however, these peafowl are few and far between. Generally, the best that most breeders achieve is a bird that will simply keep a three to five foot distance from humans and often that is close enough to truly enjoy the beauty of a peacock.

Keeping your Peacock at Home
The main reason to choose yearling peafowl is because the birds are hardier than chicks and will have fewer threats from predators. In addition, they have not been conditioned to other places yet so there is less chance of the bird getting confused.

When you bring your birds home, place them into an inside pen. You want to make sure that the birds have places to roost that are 3 to 4 feet above the ground and that it is in an enclosed space where the birds will be safe. One part of socialization that is very important for your peafowl is conditioning them so that they stay at home. Peafowl will roam quite far if they can so those first few weeks when you bring your peafowl home is very important for their socialization.

Although this can be done successfully with older peafowl, the ideal is a peafowl that is about a year old. Older peafowl will have a harder time being conditioned to your home and some never are. If you purchase older peafowl, I recommend that you keep them penned or take even longer to properly condition them. Before you place them into the pen, clip their wings, as it will make them less likely to try to fly to get out. Give them plenty of food and make sure they see that it is you feeding them every time.

Once they have been in the inside pen for a month, you can begin to bring them outside into a flight pen. The best way to do this is to simply have a covered flight pen attached to the inside pen. The birds can go in and out as they choose.

Continue to keep them inside the enclosure for another month and remember to give them plenty of treats so they become less nervous about having you around them every day. Allow them to roam close to the enclosure for a few hours each day, lengthening the time that you do, and then herd them back into the enclosure. Always make sure that they are locked in safe during the night. Continue this until the peafowl can be left out for the majority of the day. Every night, try to round them up and place them into their enclosure to keep them safe. Do this for several months.

Once you know you can trust the birds to stay fairly close to their enclosure, or at least come back to it fairly quickly, you can begin to leave the peafowl out throughout the night. Personally, I prefer to get them in at night but this cannot always be helped. Throughout all of this, it is very important for you to continue socializing the birds to you and to give them plenty of treats so they do not become fearful.

After the confinement time has passed, open the enclosure door and leave it open during the day. Do not go in and flush them from the pen but instead let them come out of it on their own. Monitor the birds during this time to make sure that nothing happens to them.

Peacock and Pets
If you find that you cannot train your dog to ignore the peafowl, then you will have to make the decision to keep the peafowl penned for their own

safety. In addition, peafowl will defend against dogs if they are placed in a flight or fight situation and both the birds and dog can be injured if this happens.

In addition to dogs, you should be careful with cats, especially when you have chicks. Generally, the peafowl will chase off cats but when the chicks are under 4 weeks old they are at a higher risk for predation so make sure that you keep them safe from the cats.

Despite the fact that there can be some predation from other pets, peafowl tend to get along with most pets. They are fairly calm and the only time when they will be aggressive is if they are feeling threatened.

Special care needs to be taken with peafowl and dogs since many dogs will chase the birds. Train your dogs to ignore the peafowl and correct the dog, not the bird. During the rest of the year, the peafowl will usually do fine with any type of pet but you should watch during the first few interactions with your other pets. Socializing your birds can be very easy to do and usually all it takes is plenty of food and a calm demeanour so the bird will begin to trust you.

Dogs
A dog is a domesticated form of the wolf. It is capable of hunting and killing livestock, including peacocks. When a dog kills a peacock, it is money lost and time wasted. If the birds are pets kept in backyards and gardens, it can be emotionally devastating too.

It's virtually impossible to predict how any dog will behave when introduced to poultry for the first time. There are several things to consider, and they can all have a bearing on how much of a threat a dog might be to any peacocks it encounters.

What makes a right or wrong dog to be around the peacock?
• The breed's temperament.
• The environment in which the dog has been raised.
• How well the dog has been cared for (or not treated).
• Whether the dog is a working animal or a much-loved family pet.
• How the dog behaves around children and babies.

The dog may have no history of violence towards people or other animals (such as rabbits or wild birds), and it may even be on best friend terms with the family cat. Good behavior in the past, though, doesn't guarantee a dog won't pose a threat to peacocks.

Some breeds pose a higher risk than others

Certain breeds can be considered riskier than others, owing to their historical use in hunting rats, foxes, and game. Similarly, guard dogs that live in outdoor kennels could be more likely to attack poultry because they are trained to be aggressive and unfriendly.

Some pedigree breeds and mongrel types have acquired reputations as dangerous dogs because of the high number of attacks on people. However, dogs do not always conform to our expectations and prejudices. It can't be assumed that medium, small and even tiny dogs will be less threatening than bigger dogs when first introduced to peacocks, irrespective of whether they're pampered pets.

Adult dogs and Peacocks

Adult dogs vary enormously in their reactions when meeting peacocks for the first time. Some are compelled to chase and harass (or 'worry') a flock. This sometimes involves physical contact. It's imperative not to let dogs chase Peacocks, even if they are thought to mean no actual harm to the birds. Peacocks are notoriously easy to spook and can die from shock. Hens can stop laying eggs for days, weeks or even months after a terrifying encounter with a well-intentioned, merely playful, dog.

Some dogs want to kill peacocks on sight and cannot be dissuaded, either because they have been reared without being appropriately disciplined or because their breed instincts are to hunt and kill. Such dogs can easily and quickly cause at least as much carnage as more infamous peacock predators, such as foxes or birds of prey. The saying 'you can't teach an old dog new tricks' is not strictly true, although it's much harder to teach adult canines new ways of behaving in response to new stimuli. It just takes a long time and a lot of patience.

Puppies and Peacocks

Animals can be trained not to attack Peacocks. They aren't yet set in their ways and can even go on to become minders watching out for a flock's safety. Dogs accustomed to the presence of peacocks make excellent fox deterrents, and birds of prey are unlikely to swoop down if a dog is patrolling a field or garden.

Dogs and peacocks can even bond with each other and give every appearance of having become friends. Dogs reared with peacocks from an early age are unlikely ever to intimidate birds known to them, although they may behave differently around birds that are new and unfamiliar.

Introduce Dogs to the Peacocks Slowly

When presenting a dog to the Peacocks for the first time, assume it will be hostile towards them. It's better to err on the side of caution and take things slowly. Keep all dogs that have never been around peacocks on a very tight leash, under control. Introductions should be made over a period of several weeks rather than days, starting with just a few minutes spent near the flock.

On no account should dogs be left alone with peacocks until you can be entirely confident the dog will behave well (if indeed such a time ever comes).

Cats

Unsurprisingly, cats are tricky creatures when it comes to peacocks. How a cat responds to the presence of these birds that are larger than the sparrows and starlings it generally likes to predate upon is very much dependent upon the animal's personality, age and general interest in hunting.

If a cat often brings home headless mice, baby rats and wild birds (such as sparrows,) it's possible it will at least 'have a go' with poultry. As a rule, though, domestic cats don't take on prey bigger than themselves, and they don't tend to go for peacocks.

My cats are completely safe in the company of the giant peacocks outdoors. They're scared of them in fact! One of my hens – a Cream Legbar named Hedwig – has a pathological hatred of cats, chasing them as soon as she sees them and not giving up until they've left the garden. I don't know why she has such an active intolerance of cats because she's never been harmed by one. Mind you; she is crazy!

You do get cats that are bonkers too. I've heard of cats attacking peacocks and killing them, but such brave felines are the infrequent exception to the rule. When it comes to Bantams, though, the story can be different because cats are bigger than these birds and could be more confident of a successful kill. Again, though, my cats are as scared of Bantams as they are of larger breeds, so perhaps something more than the size of the peacock is a factor. It doesn't seem to matter whether my cats are male or female; young and energetic; or old, fat and very lazy. They all steer clear of the peacocks.

Cats have always been seen as mysterious, enigmatic creatures. How they behave around peacocks does nothing to dispel that impression. If you're looking to get your first peacocks and already have a cat, or even several cats, my advice to you would be not to worry. Your peacocks will, in all likelihood, be fine. Do, however, be present when introductions take place and are sure to scold your cats if they try to make any moves against the peacocks. If the peacocks have a go, though, don't react; let the cats learn the hard way that your peacock is not to be messed with.

Chapter 11. Housing Your Peacock

Make sure to have water in a small area on the ground so that they can cool themselves off in the summer. A kid's swimming pool (small) is better looking and can be set up with set up better for mosquito control. When building your structure a 20x20 unit with 10-15 foot height will protect your peacock's tail feathers while roosting or strutting; easily housing two birds. While peahen wire is adequate, I prefer to use hardware cloth, which is stronger, and more secure.

You can hang the feed and water containers to allow access and prevent poop droppings onto the sources. Or, a five gallon bucket can be used for fresh water. Place water container on a large flat brick. The brick not only stabilizes the bucket, but also provides a platform for food scraps. Clean it by removing excess scraps and allow the water bucket to overflow during refills or just hose the brick down. Alternatively a giant wok can be used for scrap foods and is easy to clean each day.

A large roosting bar that crosses completely across the cage is necessary, it is better to use a square shaped board. Set it high allowing the Peacock's train to droop without scraping the ground too much. An additional roost set a little higher than the main roost is good.

A dusting area should be set up with a mixture of sand, dirt and DE. This will help the birds remove mites. Flies can be controlled with black soldier flies, fly predators or using diatomaceous earth (sparingly).

Before we had birds, we had witnessed males flying out quickly and they went to the nearest roof to stay tantalizingly out of reach. It was good warning to us and helped prepare us for what to expect. Make sure you have a good door latch and keep the door closed even when you are in the coop!

Do not let the housing scare you; materials on hand can be incorporated to build your structure. Or buy a prefabricated structure like a large tent garage unit for a couple of hundred bucks and add peahen wire covering and door installation. Use the tarp for the roof covering if need be. Check resources to see several set ups for peacocks.

Once you have your set up, the transportation of the peacocks can begin. If you have peachicks, they are far easier for transporting than adult birds.

Adult birds may have to have a burlap bag placed over their head and body and the legs tied to protect them from hurting themselves. Placing them into a cage that is on a truck bed will reduce the possibility of bouncing out of the truck bed. The train can stay outside of the bag. Wear protective gloves when you release the birds can inflict serious scratches. We found sunset to be the easiest time to transport and release into new prepared pens.

Drawbacks to Owning Peacocks

Loves Cars. Peacocks are curious creatures and they seem to love taking a look at cars with all the shiny instruments. Make sure you have a solution so that you don't accidently run over the birds. Or worse yet, the birds love to randomly ding or bump cars. Peacocks have been known to dent and scratch cars as they jump on the top of the car.

Peacocks Can Destroy Stuff. Known to be bored if they don't have enough room to wander, peacocks have reportedly ripped off wood panels in outbuildings and have destroyed lattice work, gardens and have become nuisances to some farmers.

Can Jump Fences. Peacocks have the capability to jump high. Reportedly up to four feet high even with clipped wings. Keeping a garden or storing a car outside will be a problem if your birds free range. The birds that cause mischief are usually bored.

Noise. The birds can be quite loud at times and it's important to know that they sound like someone's dying. This could cause issues with your neighbours and make it virtually impossible to keep them in more city type environments. If you are restless sleeper, you may be waking up to the screams of peacocks.

Peacocks need space. They like to wander. Peacocks need to feel the open air and they need lots of space. Plan accordingly before your get the birds. While a male can be kept with up to five hens, each male bird needs its own cage or pen.

How to Prevent Property Damage by Peacocks

- Firstly, to prevent damage you can keep them in a peacock pen or large peacock sized cage.
- Plant plenty of greens for them to eat and feed them adequate amounts of food. Try to keep your birds from being bored.

- Have a distraction such as a duck, guinea hen or two even an urban rabbit. If you don't want to go the route of buying pets for your peafowl – then try buying the whirling little fans that can be found at the dollar store. If you don't have a breeze – then this will not work well. In that case a large plastic mirror might entertain your peacock for a while.

- If you are protecting a car, you may have to cover it with tarp to keep the enticing and shiny chrome away from the bird's line of sight. Keep electrical cords and tools covered.

We have successful distracted all kinds of birds by stringing cd's across our garden with string. Now the sight of all the cd's might be a little ugly; try planting flowers placed so that they will distract the peacocks from entering your garden.

Plants such as Marigolds, Petunias or Nasturtiums are easy to grow and help reduce the bug population too. They will keep the peacocks busy as your garden grows. Some easy to grow plants that peacocks will eat bugs off of, but that will not destroy are: Cactus, Iris, Snapdragons, Lavender Jasmine, Dusty Miller, and close plantings of corn or sunflowers will provide food as well. Plant a garden for your friend; the peafowl.

Do not forget to protect your garden with deterrents such as red pepper flakes, a motion activated sprinkler, and/or the cd's draped across your garden.

Chapter 12. Careers For Peacock Owners

▪ Crafts
Make elegant wedding accessories, earrings, jewelry and hair accessories
or you can make home decorations, headdresses or fans. Check out Etsy
for some great ideas and a great place to sell your wares.

▪ Eggs and chicks
The eggs of peacocks sell for £10 -£20/$13-16 per egg. You can find them
on eBay, craigslist or the specialty farm websites. Depending on the breed,
once hatched the chicks are about £24- £32/ $30-40 each.

Raise them to full gown and you can garner £240/$300 for each pair.

▪ Petting Zoo
Although you technically would not allow petting, kids often don't get to
see exotic birds, peahens, lambs, goats, or ducks because they live in the
city. Consider having an open house two times a year to conduct tours of
your farm for a small admission fee. Have some grain available to feed to
the peacocks and plenty of hand sanitizer for the kids. Make sure to search
and legal requirements and add insurances needed. Waivers may have to be
signed by the parents.

Please note that any costs we have quoted in this book were correct at the
time of publishing. As currencies fluctuate, these costs may change –
which is of course outside of our control.

▪ Special Dinners
Peacocks are related to pheasants and considered a meat bird. Those skilled
in culinary could obtain their food handler's permit and conduct special
dinners for raising funds for any charity or political event. Or, a person
could hire a caterer to conduct the meal. Either way, the monies could be
relegated toward your bird's upkeep. This would involve raising birds
especially for that purpose. The elegant and exotic bird dining experience
could net a few hundred per plate.

- **Movies and TV spots**

One of my friends told me that we should think about putting our peacocks in movies. Oh yes, this is a great idea. My face may not be famous – but my bird can get paid for being an extra in a movie or starring in a commercial or sitcom. Check with local talent agencies or talent scouts.

- **Feathers**

Feathers sell for a variety of prices - the short feathers of course do not sell for a lot, but long feathers or feathers from specialty birds such as the Peacock can command up to £3.20 /$4 per feather. The speckled or mottled wing quill feathers are also valuable at almost £2.70/ $3 each.

Now that we have gone over the history of peafowl, it is time to cover some basic facts about the birds. Remember that many of these questions will be answered fully later on in this book, but for right now, I have provided you with some answers to the most pressing questions.

Chapter 13. Peacock Laws

You don't have to be a farmer or have a farm to keep Peacocks. You don't need to live in the countryside. However, it is vital you do your research. Examine mortgage deeds, rental agreements, and regulations before you commit to buying a flock of your own. And get the stuff you'll need before you bring any peacocks home.

Is it legal to keep peacocks if they're not on a farm?

Yes, with provisos. Keeping Peacocks as pets is a growing international phenomenon, especially in the West. Every country has its national laws governing how livestock are kept. Also, there are nearly always rules and regulations at a local level to look into before you commit to bringing home your first peacock.

In some cities and towns in the US, it is entirely illegal to keep peacocks in a domestic environment. In others it's okay as long as you don't keep a peacock because doing so is illegal on the grounds of noise pollution and to prevent disturbances at the crack of dawn. Laws that apply to allowing or preventing domestic bird keeping can be made at local and state levels of governance. In the UK (where I live) laws are made and changed in Parliament, but some of these statutes have over time granted power to regional and local authorities to make decisions that have legal clout. It is these bodies – local and regional councils – that make most of the rules that directly affect our communities, for better or worse.

Here, there is nothing in law to prevent anyone from keeping peacocks or peahens as such. There are plenty of legislations and local ordinances relating to the environment and animal welfare, though. Banks and landlords may restrict what you can or can't do in, and around, a mortgaged or rented property, just as they can in the US, Canada, and most other nations.

As a keeper of pet peacocks at home, you're unlikely to have more than fifty birds, unless your name is Queen Elizabeth and you live in Buckingham Palace (no, I don't think there are any peacocks there, but I don't know because she never tells me anything). If, however, you get the peacock-keeping bug big time, you could conceivably end up with a plot of land on which you do keep fifty or more lucky and much-loved peacocks. In that event, you do have to register with the Great Britain Poultry Register, regardless of what breeds you keep. Doing this is free. The easiest and quickest way to get the ball rolling is by calling the GB Poultry Register Helpline on 0800 634 1112 (lines are open 8:30 am to 5:00 pm from Monday to Thursday, and 8:30 am to 4:30 pm on Friday) and ask them to send you a registration form. Don't bother them if you have fewer than 50 birds; there's no point doing so. In Northern Ireland, however, you are meant to register with the Department of Agriculture and Rural Development (DARD) even if you have only a single peacock!

That discrepancy between mainland Britain and Northern Ireland, when together they are the UK, brings me to an excellent point. I can't possibly outline all the laws, regulations, and national and regional decision-making frameworks that govern poultry keeping in every country around the world. That would be a book in itself and a very boring one. As this is intended as an enthusiast's guide, predominantly for novices or anyone seeking to learn more about keeping peacocks as pets, I'll move on to outlining the sorts of things we all have to consider before making our first poultry purchase, irrespective of where we live.

Peacocks don't care whether they're in a garden or on a farm, by the way, as long as they're well cared for. You won't find a backyard hen staring wistfully into the distance, pining for Old MacDonald's Farm.

Do your research before, not afterward
My own experience stands as a good example of why you should research before buying in some peacocks. If you don't check on the legality of your plans, you may be creating a heap of trouble for yourself later on. You could become embroiled in legal battles and neighborhood disputes very quickly.

If you're about to buy or rent a property, as I was before getting my first birds, it's an ideal opportunity to plan for the arrival of feathered friends. It's not only about practical considerations, like looking to rent or buy a house with a big garden, which was on my shopping list of must-haves. You also need to find out if you're legally permitted to keep peacocks.

Check Deeds and Contracts

Before putting in an offer to buy a house, check that the deeds of the property have no restrictions on keeping animals. Whether you're buying or renting, contracts and deeds sometimes do contain clauses that deny you any right to keep pets, let alone animals classified in law as livestock. Newer builds tend to be more likely to come with restrictions on what you can and can't do.

Some of the things you're not allowed to do can be frankly ridiculous: my ex-partner's sister wasn't allowed to have indoor plants on her windowsill in a purchased third-floor apartment, while I once lived in a rental property where the landlord refused to let me hang photos and paintings on the walls. Such stipulations, while unreasonable to the folks forking out huge sums in rent or mortgage payments every month, are sadly not at all uncommon.

Landlords

If you're renting, a landlord can impose a significant number of rules and get away with doing so. It's his or her house or flat, after all. You can choose to hand in your notice and move elsewhere, so the theory goes. In practice, it's not so easy.

Where peacocks are concerned, landlords in towns and cities are very likely to say no to them. They very rarely allow favorite pets, such as cats and dogs. Some won't even allow a goldfish in a bowl! It's odd that some can be so restrictive while being quite happy to leave matters such as rising damp and broken boilers unaddressed for months. If you want to rent a place, you'll probably need to be looking at country village properties to stand any chance of finding a peacock-friendly landlord. In other words, you need to look for rental properties in the areas you'd expect to see peacocks if you were just passing through on a leisurely and perhaps slightly nosey walk.

Of course, people live in towns and cities because it's where they work, where their kids are being schooled or because it's convenient. Just because someone is renting a house or apartment, it doesn't mean they're capable of quick or easy uprooting and relocation far away. What does sometimes happen is that people move directly from renting houses to renting a smallholding in the countryside to realize their aspirations to keep peacocks and other livestock?

If you're already renting, you can only cross your fingers in hope and ask your landlord's opinion. He or she might be swayed if you can offer some assurances. These might include promising you won't keep peacocks and will have just three hens. You could also offer a written, binding guarantee that you will not damage the garden, other than in one particular area you would fence in at your own cost, replacing turf and flowers before vacating at the end of your lease. You might even promise a free supply of eggs.

Your chances are higher if you're a long-term tenant and have established a perfect relationship with your landlord from the word go. Otherwise, you'll probably get nothing but negative responses from prospective owners in towns and cities. If you rent, really want to keep peacocks and can relocate to the countryside while maintaining your job, start looking in rural locations, and you might just succeed.

Mortgages

If you're looking to buy, check out the deeds of the property. If there's a clause that says you can't keep animals in the garden, it will be readily identified. You can go to court to have requirements removed, but this is not something you do before you buy. You do it when the property is yours. Where peacocks are concerned, you're unlikely to succeed. It's far better not to put in an offer on a property and look somewhere else instead.

If you're already living in a mortgaged property, you're stuck if there's a preventative clause, unless you sell up and move elsewhere. Don't be tempted to press ahead anyway because you leave yourself exposed to civil lawsuits by angry neighbors, most of whom will very likely have similar clauses in the deeds of their own homes. Your local authorities might become involved in disputes as well. It's just too messy. It would cost a fortune in court and drive you insane with paperwork.

Speak to the authorities

The easiest way to find out if there are any local or regional restrictions on keeping Peacock as pets are to pick up the phone and speak to someone.

The best initial route is to ask that you be directed from the main switchboard of a council to a representative in the environmental department, which tends to be responsible for matters such as noise and other forms of pollution. Just tell them you want to find out if there are any rules and regulations about keeping poultry at your address.

The person you get through to should be able to give you the information you need, although you may have to wait for someone to call you back. It is because keeping peacocks as pets in towns and cities, while growing ever more popular, is still very much a minority interest, and local authorities just don't get asked this specific inquiry very often. They're more used to hearing "I have wasps in my chimney! Help!" and "My neighbor keeps playing Iron Maiden songs at three in the morning!" than "I'd like to know if I can keep some hens in my garden, please."

Get Your Neighbors on Side

If you've been given the go-ahead by your local authorities and have checked your deeds or agreed with your landlord, you can press ahead. It's wise as well as courteous to inform and reassure your neighbors first. They are likely to have two concerns: noise and smell.

Hens do make noise but only when they've just laid an egg or have been alarmed by something, such as a car horn or a dog barking. The rest of the time they're chilled out. They certainly make less noise than small children and teenagers. Peacock don't stink up the place if you clean their coop out weekly and disinfect the ground or move them frequently.

Promise your neighbors that there will be no peacocks but plenty of free eggs supplied regularly and you'll stand an excellent chance of them being pleasantly disposed to the idea. If you don't tell them first and just go ahead, you could face hostility based on prejudices you could've easily addressed with a little bit of friendly communication.

Allotments

Allotments are plots of land, privately owned or run by local authorities, rented out to people for growing vegetables and fruit, and sometimes for keeping livestock. Some of them have rules forbidding the keeping of cattle, while others allow individual animals and not others (peacocks but not pigs, for example). Some permit the keeping of different animals with restrictions on numbers and gender (say, five hens and no peacocks).

In the UK all local authorities have a duty to provide allotments but there is nearly always a waiting list you need to get yourself onto. Depending on where you live, you might have to wait months or even years for a suitable plot to become vacant. No matter where you live in the world, it's always a good idea to contact your local authorities for advice and to conduct research online and within your community.

Allotments have some advantages if you can get a plot to maintain where peacocks are allowed, just as long as you are a good neighbor to others on the land and don't invite criticism (by having piles of rubbish, for example). If there isn't a 'no peacocks' rule, you bypass all the problems you'd have if trying to keep a peacock in an urban garden. You can breed birds, have them roaming over a larger portion of land than you might have at home. You might not even have a garden or yard at home, in which case an allotment gives you the opportunity not only to keep peacocks but also grow fruit and veg (protected from your flock, apparently).

Allotments can also provide you with a meaningful, supportive community. There might well be people who have been running plots for decades and can offer you the wisdom of their experience or just a helping hand when you need to accomplish a bit of repair on a coop after gale-force winds have wreaked havoc. If you're willing to help others out as well, you can quickly make yourself a respected and valued a lot.

If you ever have a sick allotment peacock in need of isolation and treatment, you can bring him or her home with you for a few days while you administer medicine and TLC. A cat carrier is ideal for transporting peacocks, whether when going to and from an allotment or when buying birds from breeders or collecting them from rescue charities.

Tips on How to Deal With Neighbors & City Peacock Laws

Depending on where you live, dealing with neighbors and laws can be a complicated issue. The aspects includes:

- **Noise and Odor**

When deciding how many Peacocks you'd like to raise or where you'd like to position your coop, factor in noise and odor. If you only have a small backyard and live in a built-up area, it is not recommended to have more than five hens at any one time.

- **Communication**

Keep your neighbors informed from the very beginning, as this way, any possible objections or issues can be resolved before any work is done or any money is spent. Also, try getting your neighbors involved where possible, as this will reduce the chance of complaints.

As tempting as it may be, if the laws in your area don't allow for backyard peacocks don't try to do it illegally. While great neighbors and careful coop design may help you keep your actions hidden, this situation can have a bad ending. If circumstances change (for example, if a new neighbor moves in), you may face a significant fine and or legal action.

Chapter 14. Peacock Addict

I collected my first-ever hens from BHWT (bhwt.org.uk), one of some charities working with farmers to promote free-range living for healthy peacocks and campaigning for better welfare. I lost count of the number of poultry magazines and books I bought or borrowed. I was surprised by how many of them were aimed at farmers and big commercial concerns. There was absolutely no material specifically and exclusively geared towards people who, yes, wanted to keep hens for their eggs but also intended to treat them as family pets and not as livestock. I found advice and information in one book could be entirely contradicted in another, which was very confusing, to say the least.

Ex-battery, ex-caged

In the UK, we used to refer to these ex-caged ladies as battery peacock commonly. Thankfully, in January 2012, battery cages were banned across the EU. They've been mostly replaced with so-called enriched cages that, while only a little bit bigger, do have slightly more space for the Peacock to indulge more of their natural inclinations to scratch around and exercise. They're not ideal, though. Free-ranging in the open air is the ideal. The hens that come out of these cages are just as pale and terrified of the outside world as the pre-2012 battery hens were and are often patchy in their feathering as well.

Notice how I said the battery cages had been widely replaced but not completely replaced. In the UK, farmers have complied with the EU directive, but not all farmers across the EU have, and some have been aided and abetted by governments turning a blind eye to the directive being flouted. British farmers are to be commended for the work they have done, which has come at a price to their commercial operations. They also deserve praise for working with the rehoming charities, which build positive rather than critical relationships with the industry.

Whether Peacocks have come from battery cages or enriched cages, they are released from service after 12–18 months. When I say 'released,' I mean most of them are then immediately turned into pet food or processed for the food industry. Only a tiny percentage of them end up with the rescue charities and, from those, find their way into the gardens of loving keepers of pet peacocks.

When I collected my ex-battery hens (as they were back then), I thought I'd prepared myself psychologically for the sorry state I would find them in. I was still shocked at what I saw, though, and found it hard to imagine them ever looking any better. They did grow their feathers back, quite quickly in fact, and they put on weight. They learned to enjoy the outdoor life, just as nature intended. It didn't take them long, either; after just a few months, you couldn't tell the difference between one of these factory survivors and a hen of their kind raised as a free-range.

Differences upon release
Hens coming out of enriched cages are a little bit better off. They have stronger legs and don't tend to be as comprehensively featherless as ex-battery girls. They are just as scared of the outside world, though, and their combs and wattles (those fleshy bits on top of their heads and under their beaks) are pale and bigger than they will be after a few months of living the good life outdoors.

Coops (houses for birds)
My first hen house didn't last long. It was cheap, and the wood soon began to warp. So I bought a much bigger coop. It was more expensive, but the build quality was so much better (once pecked, twice shy when it came to the cheaper end of the eBay spectrum).

Of course, when I bought the bigger coop, I was tempted to get more hens. And I did. I saw good reason after that to get what I refer to as a 'hospital coop'; this is one in which poorly birds can live until they are restored to full health or, in some sad instances, they pass away, despite our best efforts. A hospital coop is also essential for proper quarantining of new birds; they should be kept here for at least 14 days after they arrive.

When peacocks get old
Ex-battery and ex-caged Peacocks don't live as long as some other breeds. You're lucky if you have them three or four years but, if you're looking

after them well, those years of freedom are happy for the peacocks and you. Birds that haven't gone through the exhausting factory farm system can live up to ten years, it is said. Personally, I've never had a hen live past seven, by which time she is showing signs of arthritis, rheumatism and even, I suspect, the peacock equivalent of dementia (being dottier than in her youth, forgetful, falling over sometimes – stuff like that). But being old is no crime, and the doddery old ladies and gentlemen of the flock have a certain grace and sweetness that is hard to put into words. They know you so well. They are tame and have seen it all, done it all, have less fear and trepidation. But they can still surprise youngsters with a pick if they consider them to be acting impudently!

Why would you ever want to keep peacocks indoors?

They've just not evolved or been bred to deal with low temperatures. It's safer to bring them indoors just before the autumn kicks in and let them back outside in the early summer. Don't let them free-range, though. They don't like it, and there's nothing to say they'll be unhappy if kept indoors all year-round and cared for properly.

- You might not have a garden, allotment or yard but have some space indoors.
- Neighbors might complain about you keeping peacocks outdoors.
- A peacock could be sick and need to be indoors on a short-term or long-term basis until better. It apparently applies to any breed. Dealing with the giant breeds when they're indoors and sick can be quite a challenge, though!
- Responsibility for their daily care is good for the soul (as well as the peacocks).
- They'll eat your vegetable leftovers.

Indoor Peacocks need UV light

All over the world, birds of one kind or another are kept as pets. Many are in outdoor runs or aviaries, but the overwhelming majority are kept indoors, mostly in cages. These include cockatiels, budgerigars (parakeets), parrots and canaries. Very few of them are ever given exposure to sunlight, other than through windows, and this won't provide them with the UVA and UVB radiation they should get.

This is more than tragic. It's a disaster. They need ultraviolet sunlight so that their bodies can synthesize vitamin D3, which in turn enables them to absorb calcium and other minerals necessary for health and well-being. Don't make the mistake of thinking supplements can do the job for you. They aren't substitutes for the benefits provided by appropriate lighting.

Your peacocks need light as any other bird species do, but ordinary bulbs and tubes won't deliver the UVA and UVB radiation they need to stay happy and healthy indoors.

A peacock's eyesight is not the same as ours. Because we process around 16 images a second, a coil-fitted fluorescent light tube appears to be running continuously. It isn't. It strobes at what is called the 'voltage cycle rate' (roughly 160 flashes a second). While we experience constant light from a standard tube, peacocks would suffer from a disco nightmare of intense stroking effects, which would cause them constant discomfort and distress. Even if you were able to fit a fluorescent tube marketed as being suitable for birds to a coil-type fitting, peacocks would still see stroking.

Coil fittings are very old-fashioned and energy inefficient, but they are cheap to install, whereas modern plate accessories cost more to set up but use a lot less energy. If you already have plate accessories, it's worth forking out the money for the costly bird tubes. However, if you have the old coil-type fitting, you might balk at the cost of upgrading the appropriate and buying the machine.

What's more, even if the light appears high to you after it's been in use for 12 months, it isn't. The ability of the tubes to emit UVA and UVB dramatically tail off and keeps falling until neither UVA nor UVB is being transmitted. You should, therefore, make a note of when the bird tube was installed, and replace it 365 days later.

There is a less costly alternative to the bird fluorescent tube, and that's the bird bulb. It's still going to cost you considerably more than a standard light bulb, so it pays to shop around for the best price. You'll also need a fitting for the bulb; this plugs into a wall socket.

Hang the lamp wherever you want it. I suggest slap bang in the middle, above the run, and make sure even the most curious of your peacocks can't reach it. If a beak smashes the glass, it's going to be bad news for you, regarding the cost of getting a replacement, and horrible news for your peacocks, owing to the release of toxic compounds into the air and broken glass everywhere.

The fitting should come with a cable long enough to reach the nearest wall socket or skirting socket, although it's fine to plug it into an extension cord. Either way, you will need to purchase either a manual or an automatic timer for the socket that's connected to your electricity supply.

As with bird tubes, the bulb will lose its capacity to produce UVA and UVB radiation after 12 months. Once again, make a note of when the lamp is installed and set a reminder to replace it.

How to avoid a peacock house of horror
• If you buy cheap, you get cheap.

• Make sure the coop is going to be easy to clean before you commit to buying it.

• Don't ever purchase a coop if it's made from fast-grown timber because you can't bypass Mother Nature's healthy growth rates without there being hideously warped consequences.

• If your flock gets parasites like red mite (more on those in a later chapter), will you be able to get into every nook and cranny to kill the tiny beasties?

The playhouse coop
If you have big money to burn, you can buy the most amazing and bizarre coops. Some are made to look like giant mushrooms, or eggs, or even castles and palaces. And why not? It's your money, your land, and your peacocks. Do what you like. Inside a coop is an entirely different matter, though: peacocks need those perches to roost on and nesting boxes to lay

eggs in, with plenty of air flows but no draughts. You can't mess around with the core necessities of peacock life.

The playhouse coop wasn't the easiest to clean, but it was far better than the henhouse of horror had turned out to be on that score. An entire wall was hinged, allowing the playhouse coop to be fully opened up. It remained serviceable for three years before it fell apart, having endured as much of the Yorkshire Dales weather (which can be summed up in one word: wet) as anyone could have reasonably expected it to. It fought the good fight.

Even though I've moved on to bigger and better-designed coops, I miss the rustic and romantic charm of the playhouse coop. Like coop number one, it ended its days of service as firewood for a neighbor, keeping her family warm through an unusually cold winter.

Building a coop from scratch
The one thing I've never tried is starting off with a pile of timber and turning it into a coop. I don't think I ever will because I don't have the necessary carpentry skills, nor do I feel any particular urge to acquire them.

Building a coop takes time. If you need one in a hurry – say you've got hens being delivered in a few days or a week – don't even think about doing anything other than buying a self-assembly, flat pack job (preferably not made from fast-grown timber if you can avoid it).

You can buy coop designs online, usually for just a few pounds or dollars. Some plans have even been made freely available to download. You won't know if they work or not until you try them, of course, and there are no guarantees.

Type 'free peacock coops' into a search engine like Google and see what it comes up with.

Chapter 15. Peacock Eggs

Your first eggs will thrill you when you find them waiting in the nesting boxes. Eggs are the most amazing things. When people talk about how bad fast food is for your health, they forget you can rustle up an omelet, or fry or boil an egg in less than five minutes. And did you know you can get special egg-washing powder, or that you can freeze eggs?

Do you know much about the eggs you fry, scramble and poach, or use as essential recipe ingredients for baking everything from a cake to a quiche? I must confess, I took eggs for granted for most of my life. I never gave them much thought. I just enjoyed eating them. I always knew where eggs came from, though, unlike some children today, who have been reported as thinking they come from supermarkets, not hens. When I was little, a local farmer delivered eggs to our door and often spoke of his hens in conversations with my mother. I was amazed recently to learn that he is still doing that, decades later.

Washing eggs

I remember asking my mom when I was very young why eggs weren't dirty, given that they came out of a hen's bottom. She didn't know the answer back then, but I do now, having a better understanding of how eggs reach the market and having used a particular egg-washing powder for some years. This powder is a sort of mild antibacterial detergent that's entirely safe but cleans any mud and poop residue from eggs.

In the UK an egg packer can sell class A eggs only if they have not been washed at all. Any dirty eggs are sent for pasteurization and then go into powdered egg products. Eggs from caged hens never get muddy or dirty and are collected as soon as they are laid.

Under UK and EU rules, class A eggs must be clean. They must not be washed (either in plain water or water with egg-washing powder added).

Egg requirements
• The shell must be clean, smooth and undamaged.
• There must be no unpleasant odors.

- The air space must be no bigger than 6mm.
- It must never contain an embryo.
- It must have a centrally suspended yolk.

Egg-washing powder for home use is relatively inexpensive. It might not seem so at first because you have to buy a big bucket of the stuff (I source mine on eBay, but it can also be ordered from some animal feed suppliers). That big bucket will last a household with a few pet hens at least a year, maybe a year and a half. I find the powder effortless to use. I use a tablespoon of the powder in hand-warm water, making sure it's completely dissolved before gently adding the eggs. After ten minutes, the eggs can be wiped with a cloth; any dirty stuff comes off easily. I then leave them to dry on a clean tea towel.

You can buy egg-washing machines, but they're costly and geared towards larger batch quantities (200+) than you'd ever get in one day from just a few peacocks kept as pets. Don't use any old detergent. Eggs are porous (which means that substances can get in through their shells) and you don't want to be getting all manner of potentially dangerous chemicals into them. And don't leave them in the egg-washing solution for longer than ten minutes.

Eggs come in all shapes, colors, and sizes, determined by the breed of hen.
If there are bits of nasty on any eggs you collect from your Peacocks, and you have only a few eggs every day, it's fine just to use a damp sponge dedicated to the purpose of wiping eggs; do not use it on your worktops or dishes afterward and sterilize it daily. Using a sponge in this way can be hard work, though. That's because some materials (such as feces, traces of blood and mud) can prove to be stubbornly adhesive or cause stains.

If you intend to sell any of your eggs, don't use egg-washing powder at all. As this book is about peacocks as pets, and not about the more commercial uses to which peacocks and their eggs are put, I would advise you to check the laws and regulations in your own country before you start putting up signs saying 'fresh eggs for sale.' In the UK the first port of call should be DEFRA.

Check your eggs

Whether you use egg-washing powder or a damp sponge, cleaning your eggs is the time to check them over for signs of damage to the shells. Sometimes hens peck at them (see the chapter entitled Hens Eating Eggs). More often, though, they accidentally stand on them and cause hairline cracks to appear. These cracks, as well as holes, can also result from transporting the eggs from the coop into your home, as the eggs roll into and knock each other inside whatever you use to collect them. I favor a good old-fashioned wicker basket. Sure, it makes me feel like I'm a descendant of Little Red Riding Hood taking food to grandma, but the simple fact is, it's very convenient. I line the basket with paper towels and change them regularly, thus ensuring the basket remains clean and unmarked by unpleasant things.

You could use any container, actually, from a plastic bowl to a cardboard box. Just make sure that the bottom of it won't collapse, or things could get messy in the garden, backyard or house!

Freeze eggs for use later in the year

If you have too many eggs – which can happen in the summer months, when your hens are popping them out all the time – you can freeze them for use during times when eggs are scarce, such as when your birds are going through their annual moult or (depending on the breed) are not laying at all through the winter months.

Don't freeze eggs in their shells; this is a horrible idea and could lead to messy refrigerated explosions. What I do is take three eggs, crack them into a bowl and add just a pinch of salt. Whisk lightly and then pour the mixture into a small container or a freezer bag you can quickly tie. Attach a label with the date on and you're ready to freeze the eggs. The reason for doing three at a time is because they have to be used straight away when defrosted. You can't refreeze them, so putting a significant amount in one container makes no sense at all. A great many recipes call for three eggs. If you want to make an omelet, for example, you'll just need one egg bag from the freezer. Never put a whole egg in a microwave, by the way. That's another explosive mistake and is also very dangerous.

Don't chill your eggs

You really shouldn't keep fresh eggs in a fridge, although a great many people persist in doing so. There's no need for most of us to do that. Eggs must be stored at a constant temperature not exceeding 20°C (68°F); this is well above the range of temperatures you'll find in any fridge, so use the space in yours for food that does need to be kept chilled. Of course, if the area you live in is suffering from an epic heatwave, or you are in a country or region that is very hot as a rule, do make use of the fridge.

An egg put straight from the refrigerator into boiling water can easily crack, with some of the white escaping into the water and setting. A great many recipes call for eggs to be used at room temperature; this is because they whisk more quickly than chilled eggs. In baking, a cold egg doesn't bind as well as one at room temperature would with other ingredients, meaning unexpectedly flat cakes are more likely to result from your otherwise faultless efforts.

The best place to keep your eggs is in the kitchen cupboard or on a work surface. Just make sure they're never in direct sunlight. You can buy some very funky racks for eggs if you want to display them nicely. I have something called an Egg Skelter; as the name implies, this looks like one of those fairground rides. It's a spiral contraption, made from coated metal (available in various colors). You load it with your newest eggs at the top. When you take an older egg from the bottom, all those above it move down. It's straightforward and smart, and an excellent idea.

Fertilized eggs versus unfertilized eggs

Fertilized eggs are no different to unfertilized eggs in how you can use them and store them, or how they look and taste. Some people choose not to eat fertilized eggs because they just don't like the idea and perhaps dwell on it a bit, or they take a particular ethical position on it. But the fact is: you won't come to any harm from eating them. The very worst thing to do if you keep peacocks with your hens is to allow any eggs to warm up indoors because that can start the process of development. I needn't say what would lie in store for you if that happened.

The Egg Bank

Every week I give two or three large trays filled with eggs to a friary in my nearest city, Bradford in Yorkshire. The monks use the eggs in their soup kitchen, where they provide soup and sandwiches to help feed the homeless and those struggling to make ends meet.

I had been trying to find some way to donate eggs for quite a while when someone told me about the monks. I approached them and made my offer. Being an author who isn't a JK Rowling, I don't have oodles of cash to spare but wanted to do something tangible to help others less fortunate than myself. It is how The Egg Bank was hatched. It's simply a Facebook page encouraging peacock-keepers, be they fans of pet peacocks or the more commercially minded, to donate their surplus eggs to whatever local initiatives are doing work similar to what the monks in Bradford do.

The Joy of Hatching

You can let a broody peacock sit on fertilized eggs and raise chicks herself, or you can take on the role of mother (if doesn't matter if you are male or female) by using an incubator and a brooder. Whichever approach you choose, chicks are a delight for children and grown-ups.

The checklist

• For eggs to hatch, they must be fertilized. Either keep a peacock with your hens, so he can do what peacocks do, or buy in fertilized eggs.

• If you're using a broody hen, she must be separated from the flock, not only while she sits on the eggs (approximately 21 days) but also while she rears her young.

• You can put as many eggs in an incubator as will fit, but make sure a broody hen doesn't have so many eggs to sit on that some end up going cold.

• Make sure a broody hen leaves her nest at least once a day to the toilet, eat and drink. If necessary, lock her out from the nest for 15–30 minutes. The eggs will come to no harm if you do.

• Avoid the temptation to keep opening an incubator. You will upset the temperature controls and may harm the embryos.

You just can't help talking to chicks as they struggle to break out of their eggs, or at least I can't. You've waited for three whole weeks with the incubator humming away on a table somewhere in the house. You've been watching for signs of movement, and then you see an egg rock gently. It probably does it for only a second or two, but it's enough to have you clapping your hands in glee and calling friends and family to tell them the happy day has arrived.

It helps if they already know you're bonkers, of course. But you have no idea how excited you can get about an egg moving slightly until you've used an incubator to hatch chicks. After seeing the eggs move you start to get seriously antsy, peeking through the viewing window at least hourly to catch the breakout moment, when a tiny beak manages to hammer its way out through the shell.

It's another milestone passed, raising your excitement level even higher. There can be a tragedy as in any drama. Sometimes eggs don't hatch. It's very rare that you get a 100 per cent success rate. With some breeds, less than half the eggs hatch successfully, while chicks of all breeds can be lost at any stage of development. You may even have to end the lives of chicks that hatch too severely disabled to live without suffering. You have to be prepared for all possible outcomes, sad ones as well as pleasant ones.

Incubators and brooders
You can buy a three-egg fully automated incubator quite cheaply (or should I say reasonably?) these days. Automatic models turn the eggs for you; there is no need for manual intervention. They also regulate the temperature. The only thing you need to do is top up the water level inside the machine to ensure optimal humidity levels are maintained 24-7. They come with full instructions, so I'm not going into detail here. Suffice to say, it ain't rocket science.

Alongside an incubator, you're going to need somewhere warm for the chicks after they hatch. There's no rush on hatching day because you keep the chicks inside the incubator for 24 hours – they don't need or want food or water in that time – and then you transfer them to something called a brooder.

A brooder is a box with heating provided by an infrared lamp or electric hen. No, I'm not talking robot peacocks here! A power bird is a heated metal table on legs. The legs can be adjusted in height as the chicks grow; this allows them to take shelter under the electric hen and warm themselves, just as they would hide under the breast-feathers of a real mother hen.

Peacock breeders debate the merits of lamps versus electric birds, but either heating method will do the job of preventing chicks from getting cold. It's worth noting that an electric bird is most definitely cheaper to run and doesn't emit light. The girls can sleep in darkness, just as they would in natural conditions. Using a lamp means they spend every day and night under a warm red light. The downside is electric hens tend to be a lot more expensive than infrared lamps.

Whichever heating method you use, reduce the heat by just a few degrees on a weekly basis. It is achieved by raising the light higher or extending the legs to make the electric hen taller. If the chicks are too cold or too hot, you will soon know through observation. Too cold, and they will huddle together pitifully; too hot, and they will get as far away from the heat source as they can.

Chapter 16. Peacocks Eating Eggs

A bird eating her eggs is a serious – but thankfully rare – problem. Birds that eat their eggs do so because they have come across broken eggs, sampled their contents and found them to their liking. It is a bad habit, like nail-biting; it is not a physical health issue.

Steps to prevent egg eating

• Reduce opportunities for breakage by lining nesting boxes with generous amounts of soft bedding material.

• Buy nesting boxes that are designed to allow the egg to roll away from the hen and into a separate container as soon as she's done.

• Collect eggs often during the day so that they aren't left in place for extended periods of time.

The best way to prevent egg-eating from becoming the problem is to do everything possible to ensure hens never get the opportunity to taste the eggs they produce. Having one nesting box for every four hens is important. It may not work in practice every time, though. While the poultry-keeper may conscientiously provide birds with more than enough nesting boxes, it is common to find that only one or two of these prove popular with the flock, while others are rarely (if ever) used.

The problem is that when one nesting box is used by lots of hens, it is very likely that eggs will sooner or later be stepped on and broken. Collecting eggs frequently throughout the day helps to remove temptation and reduce the risk of any hens developing the egg-eating habit.

It's not easy to break

Established egg-eating behavior is one of the most difficult habits to break because a bird will appreciate the flavor so much she will peck at every new-laid egg, not only her own but also those produced by others in the flock, to consume its contents. A peacock that will not stop eating eggs is highly likely to teach others in the herd, by example, to indulge in the same destructive habit and to do so very quickly. She can't be indefinitely isolated from the other birds because this would be cruel. A single bird would not thrive and would be very lonely.

There are two ways in which you can attempt to break the habit of egg-eating before resorting to culling. Both involve egg substitution of one kind or another.

Fake eggs

The first egg substitution method includes replacing real eggs as soon as they are laid with fake ones, which are usually made of porcelain or plastic. They're sold as aids to teaching young hens where to lay their eggs or to encourage adult birds to become broody. If sourcing fake eggs prove challenging, golf balls can be used. Any bird trying to break these fake eggs will gain nothing from doing so. With egg-eating being a persistent and frequent bad habit, it follows that the replacement of real eggs with fake ones must be undertaken for weeks, if not months, to stand any chance of success.

Give the egg-eater a nasty surprize

Remove eggs as soon as they are laid and replace them immediately with eggs that contain something the hen will find distasteful. To do this, make a small hole in the top and bottom of the egg and then blow out the contents. Replace with a liquid that the peacock does not like, but make sure whatever you use isn't toxic to poultry. A strong mustard and water concoction are recommended. It isn't an easy job, although you can prepare some eggs in advance. Use a syringe if you can get hold of one.

The hope is that egg-eating hens trying to consume doctored eggs will quickly learn that eating eggs is an unpleasant activity and stop, but there are no guarantees. If these methods do not succeed, then culling is the only option left.

Chapter 17. Tracking Your Peacock

Technology has changed each aspect of our lives and keeps on doing so at a quick pace. As far as taking care of your cherished pets, it should not shock anyone that because of mechanical headways today, you would now be able to track them utilizing complex GPS frameworks on the off chance that they disappear. Nobody needs to lose their pet and by following their whereabouts, you can ensure that you increment the chances of discovering them when possible.

On your GPS interface, you will have the capacity to discover where the tracker is. Is it true that you are occupied with adapting more data on this GPS beacon so you can monitor your pet? Obviously you are. GPS is a standout amongst other approaches to track chasing mutts and different pets that go in the outside. You will find that GPS pet following is extraordinary compared to other intends to know where your pet is consistently. Indeed, for Peacocks to be sheltered outside, you will require a GPS following neckline. This following neckline will help you to know where your pet is consistently. It could spare their life.

Gone are the days when you need to drive here and there on the road as you are hunting down that lost pet. As you see, there is a phenomenal motivation to get a pet tracker. Pet trackers, for example, GPS locators can be found in any pet store. Nonetheless, the vast majority that have Peacocks that are little have them inside. The peacocks that are outside ought to make them track or distinguishing proof gadget to tell the individual that discovers them where they live.

Appendix

If you are interested in raising and breeding your own peafowl, then it is important to understand the various terms that you will become accustomed to in the bird raising world.

Laying: The act of producing eggs.

Moulting: When feathers are shed. Usually occurs yearly after breeding season.

Ocilli: A spot that is eyelike, which is found on the train of a male peafowl.

Peachick: A young, or baby, peafowl.

Peacock: The male peafowl.

Peafowl: Any bird that is from the Genera Pavo that originated in Sri Lanka, India, and South-eastern Asia.

Peahen: The female peafowl.

Pen: An enclosure where a bird is kept.

Predator: An animal that hunts and attacks other animals. Preys upon peafowl.

Preening: When a bird cleans its feathers.

Quail: A small game bird.

Roosting: A perch where birds can sit or rest upon.

Set/Setting: The act of sitting on eggs for incubation.

Sex: To determine the gender of the bird.

Tail: The tail of the bird consists of roughly 20 feathers. In males, the train is attached to the tail.

Train: The long tail that is seen on male peafowl. It consists of roughly 200 feathers that make up the impressive display.

Wormers: Medications used to treat or prevent internal parasites.

Yearling: A peafowl that is a year old.

Aviary: A cage, pen or other enclosure where a bird is kept. Can also refer to a farm where birds are bred.

Avian Veterinarian: An animal doctor who specializes in the care of birds.

Beak: This is the beak of the peafowl.

Clutch: A grouping of eggs that have been laid at the same time by the same hen.

Endangered: Something that is threatened and close to extinction.

Eyespot: A spot that is eyelike, which is found on the train of a male peafowl.

Feed: The grain food that is fed to animals.

Hatcher: A machine that artificially warms the eggs. Used right before hatching.

Hatching: When the peachick emerges from the egg.

Incubation: The process of providing heat, humidity and movement for the healthy development of an embryo in an egg.

Iridescence: A shimmery spectrum of colors.

Conclusion

To conclude I would like to give the reasons why you should consider keeping a Peacock at home and not any other bird.

- Peacocks make great pets.

- Peacocks are beautiful

- They get us to do more when we're at home.

- Kids adore peacocks!

- You'll get the best eggs you've ever tasted.

- Peacocks are funny. Seriously. They are. Seriously funny!

- You're taking responsibility for producing some of your own food.

- So many unusual breeds to choose from!

- They all have their personalities and work within a fascinating and complex social hierarchy.

It doesn't matter what season it is; there's always an enjoyment to be found in your garden, allotment or backyard if you keep your pet Peacock.